After the Storm

After the Storm

Bob Walker and the East Bay Regional Park District

WITHDRAWN

WRITTEN BY CHRISTOPHER BEAVER

WILDERNESS PRESS · BERKELEY, CA

After the Storm: Bob Walker and the East Bay Regional Park District

1st EDITION November 2007

Text copyright © 2007 by Christopher Beaver
Bob Walker photographs copyright © 2007 by Natural Sciences Division, Oakland Museum of California
Map on p. 173 courtesy East Bay Regional Park District with additional design by Bart Wright

Library of Congress Card Number: 2007060409
ISBN: 978-0-89997-453-8
UPC: 7-19609-97453-6

Manufactured in China

Published by: **Wilderness Press**
1200 5th Street
Berkeley, CA 94710
(800) 443-7227; FAX (510) 558-1696
info@wildernesspress.com
www.wildernesspress.com

Visit our website for a complete listing of our books and for ordering information.

Library of Congress Cataloging-in-Publication Data

Walker, Bob, 1952–1992.
  After the storm : Bob Walker and the East Bay Regional Park District / [photography by Bob Walker].—1st ed.
    p. cm.
  ISBN 978-0-89997-454-5 (cloth)—ISBN 978-0-89997-453-8 (pbk.) 1. East Bay Regional Park District (Calif.)—Pictorial
works. 2. East Bay (Calif.)—Pictorial works. 3. Landscape—California—East Bay Regional Park District—Pictorial works.
4. Landscape—California—East Bay—Pictorial works. 5. Walker, Bob, 1952–1992. 6. Photographers—California—East
Bay—Biography. 7. Environmentalists—California—East Bay—Biography. 8. East Bay Regional Park District (Calif.)—
Environmental conditions. 9. East Bay (Calif.)—Environmental conditions. I. Title.
  F868.E22W35 2007
  917.94'6—dc22
                                                                                                    2007060409

Contents

Pleasanton Ridge Trail

Pleasanton Ridge Regional Park
East of Pleasanton, California
November 1985

Welcome

Beauty is said to lie in the eye of the beholder.

Through this book one can experience extraordinary beauty through the eyes of Bob Walker.

His photographs offer a spiritual vision of the East Bay landscape and of the lands of the East Bay Regional Parks. They capture beauty, unique features, and the challenges we all face in the preservation of nature's treasures.

Bob Walker adopted the East Bay Regional Parks, and like a pied piper played a kind of visual music that calls to us to embrace these lands.

On each page of this book, he still beckons us to see the land as he captured it in these insightful photographs and as he once again challenges our spirits to protect the natural treasures of the East Bay and beyond.

Pat O'Brien
General Manager
East Bay Regional Park District

Find something outside yourself that is yourself.
Then devote yourself to it with all your heart.

Bob Walker

Maguire Peak

Sunol Regional Wilderness
South of Pleasanton, California
October 1985

Robert John Walker (1952–1992), a 15-year resident of San Francisco's Haight-Ashbury district, discovered the meaning he sought for his life – that equivalence outside himself – in the open countryside around San Francisco Bay.

What Ansel Adams and other photographers discovered in the distant Sierra Nevada or even more remote locales, Walker found in his own backyard.

In fact, almost all of the photographs in this book were taken no more than an hour's drive from downtown San Francisco, Oakland, or San Jose – in the East Bay region, a distance of 60 miles from San Francisco Bay across Alameda and Contra Costa counties until the landscape flattens into California's Central Valley.

Bob Walker, as he was known personally and professionally, began his artistic career as a painter and conceptual artist at Ohio's Oberlin College in the 1970s. In tune with the times, he produced bold silkscreened prints and collage sculptures preserved in clear plastic.

After graduation in 1974, Walker set his sights on San Francisco. He made the journey west in a battered red VW Bug overflowing with plants, favorite snapshots, and his best friend, a dog named in Walker's often bemused manner, "Dog."

After a brief apprenticeship as a weekend hiker and occasional photographer, Walker would devote the final ten years of his life to photography and the protection of open space.

Revealed through Walker's eyes, the hills and grasslands of the San Francisco's East Bay region stand forth in all their majesty and power, qualities perhaps overlooked by long-term residents or those passing through on their way to more far-flung destinations.

As he shifted his focus to serious photography, Walker began to realize that he could make an important contribution to the growing debate over open-space preservation. Very simply, he decided to show ordinary people and government officials what the land actually looked like.

Author and curator Ellen Manchester identified the impact this activism had on Walker and on his work:

Walker began to emphasize the use of his photographs to educate the public and to advocate specific land-use policies. As his vision became more precise in intent, it grew in power, capturing the open landscape in its surprising beauty and its disheartening destruction.

Walker understood quite well the demands such presentations made on the quality of his photography. "To involve the public," he once said, "you have to make each of your pictures a thousand times more spectacular than what you might see on the most exquisite day – otherwise you'll never convey even one-tenth of what it feels like to be out there on the dullest gray day when nothing's going on."

Indeed, many of Walker's finest images were made specifically to illustrate the talks he gave to county supervisors, business associations, Boy Scout troops, and virtually any other group that would have him.

One fellow photographer observed that "the slide-show may well have been his truest art form."

By spending time on the land not because the work demanded it, but because he got a kick out of being out there, Walker managed to capture what he saw, and more importantly, what he felt about the East Bay.

The lasting value of Walker's commitment may be found in the words of Pat O'Brien, General Manager, East Bay Regional Park District:

The game will be over in 20 years. All the undeveloped open space of the East Bay will either be protected or developed over the course of the next two decades. By drawing on Walker's work and inspiration, we have a fighting chance to protect this extraordinary landscape for generations to come.

As a political activist, Walker understood that the idea of storms applied not only to the weather in which his photographs found their most dramatic expression. The image of the storm also applies to the society in which we live – from environmental degradation to such modern-day plagues as the AIDS epidemic that would ultimately take Walker's life.

If such ominous clouds characterize our society all too well, Walker demonstrated by his activism and in his photography that as close as we live to despair and darkness, we are equally close to light and hope.

As a tribute to Bob Walker and to the open space he so cherished, we have entitled this presentation of Walker's photographs *After the Storm*.

Legacy Olive Grove

Pleasanton Ridge Regional Park
West of Pleasanton, California
November 1984

Purchased by the East Bay Regional Park District as an
addition to Pleasanton Ridge Regional Park in 1986.
Ohlone Wilderness and Sunol Regional Wilderness can
be seen in the distant hills. San Francisco Water District's
San Antonio Reservoir lies at their feet in the center.

To Bob Walker's first written inquiry in 1981 about the East Bay Regional Park District and future land acquisition, the official response might well have begun by explaining that the district is nearly unique in the United States – a freestanding, independent governmental organization founded in 1934 by citizens interested in preserving open space. The District's mission is to acquire and manage a system of interconnected parklands while balancing public recreational use with the protection and preservation of natural and cultural resources. It was a philosophy Walker embraced without hesitation.

Although his photography focused on the East Bay, Walker lived in a simple garden apartment in San Francisco's Haight-Ashbury and worked as an apartment manager in Berkeley, California, across from People's Park. Never one to let barriers stand in his way, Walker spent his free time roaming public – and sometimes not-so-public – open space in the East Bay. With a secondhand camera and no formal training, he took to the hills, as Walker often said, simply in search of a place to walk his dog.

As luck would have it, early in 1982 Walker happened to hike the Ohlone Wilderness with a group of people that included two Park District board members. They in turn invited Walker to present a slideshow of his photographs from the hike at a meeting of the Park District board. When Jerry Kent, one of five assistant general managers for the Park District, saw the slides, he remembers storing Walker's name in his mental Rolodex along with the simple notation, "this guy has talent."

As soon as he could manage, Kent hired Walker for the first of what would be many Park District contracts that ran from 1982 until close to Walker's death in September of 1992. The assignment was as basic as it was sweeping: create the first collection of professional photos of the parklands. Walker was in heaven. Even though the contract barely covered film, developing costs, and gas for his car, he was now a paid professional photographer.

Bob Doyle, an assistant general manager of the Park District with responsibility for land acquisition, remembers Walker often bounding into the District's Skyline Boulevard offices after a long day chasing shadows in the parklands with his camera:

> He knew he'd more than likely catch me at my desk with nobody else to intervene because he knew I always worked late. He'd rush in with one of his pictures and ask if I could explain it to him on a map. By that time of the day I'd be exhausted and brain dead, but Walker was someone who got you so excited you had no choice but to respond.

The two Bobs, Walker and Doyle, spent long hours together as Doyle taught Walker how to read maps and interpret the topography of the parks. At the end of a typical session Walker usually managed to take a few "used" maps home with him for reference purposes. In time, Walker's collection of maps would cover an entire wall of his apartment with a panorama of the entire San Francisco Bay region, a mosaic that leaned heavily in the direction of the East Bay.

As Walker increasingly understood the connection between his photographs and maps of the area, he began to wonder what could be done with the relationship between people's responses to his beautiful landscape photography and their desire to protect the land for future generations. The answer was not long in coming.

In 1986, Walker discovered a For Sale sign on the Marshall property adjacent to Morgan Territory Regional Preserve, one of Walker's favorite haunts. In that instant, a park activist was born. Walker began to lobby his contacts at the Park District to lobby the District's Board of Directors to buy the property. And he lobbied conservation organizations to lobby the Board. He shaped his presentations as carefully as he took his photographs, drawing on an instinctive, gentle touch that rested on an underlying passion and love for the land.

With a clear view of his ultimate goal, Walker was able to cut to the heart of an issue yet remain fair and civil, a politician in the best sense of the word, someone who brought people together. In late 1986, the Marshall property officially became part of Morgan Territory.

It was the first of many similar campaigns, including my own appointment to the Park District Board in 1987 and my subsequent public elections in 1988 and 1990. Walker's photographic work played a more visible role in passage of the Park District's open space acquisition bond, Measure AA, in 1988. It was, as Bob Doyle remembers it, "a unique time largely because of Walker's influence; it was a time when we managed to save the last of the best."

Throughout this time, Walker continued to foster his own acquisition schemes backed by a unique style of educational hiking.

Each hike concluded with Walker's insistence that every hiker write a postcard to public officials lobbying them to preserve more land. One especially heartfelt effort led to the purchase of the Nipper property for Pleasanton Ridge Regional Park in 1988.

To hike with Walker on a piece of land was to experience magic. He would glide effortlessly over the rockiest of trails despite his many pounds of photographic gear. Although the routes he suggested appeared spontaneous, in retrospect it seems that he must have planned each vista for maximum effect.

After Walker died, a group of friends and people with whom he'd worked on conservation issues gathered at a memorial service in Morgan Territory to recall the impact he had on our lives and to honor his legacy. Each of us seemed to be asking the same question: How had Bob Walker packed so much accomplishment into so very few years?

As we spoke, a helicopter flown by Andrew White, a Park District pilot and Walker's longtime ally in aerial photography, appeared in the sky. It lingered above a ridge and trail named by the District in Walker's honor shortly before his death. This time, White was there to scatter Walker's ashes.

As the plume of ashes descended earthward, I think we all realized that Walker had come full circle. He had saved the land and he had become the land.

Ohlone Moon

Ohlone Wilderness
South of Sunol, California
October 1987

CHAPTER ONE

Mount Diablo, The Center

Thanksgiving Day, Mount Diablo

Morgan Territory Regional Preserve
Northeast of Livermore, California
November 1987

Mount Diablo, The Center

As far back as time, distance, and memory can take us, Mount Diablo has always been the center.

For the earliest inhabitants, Mount Diablo was the point where eagle and condor came together with the mountain. There, upon its heights, Coyote created the Miwok people – the Chupcan, Julpun, Ompin, Saclan, Tatcan, and Volvon. From Diablo's summit, light was born.

At the top of the mountain, in a small concrete-enclosed visitor's center, it's possible to stand astride the physical summit. At this point in 1851, Colonel Leander Ransom, at the behest of the surveyor general for California, carved a hole in the mountain's porous rock.

Into what had once been the floor of an ancient ocean, Ransom placed a flagpole so that all could see his mark from a great distance.

From that point outward, based on the Mount Diablo base line and Mount Diablo meridian line, Ransom established what would become a right-angled grid of property lines. His survey marks the final transformation of landscape from common ownership or Spanish land grant into public and private property for a vast portion of California and most of Nevada.

Within sight of the mountain and beyond – from backyard, apartment, campsite, and lookout – all modern property boundaries in the San Francisco Bay Area, including the East Bay region, align with Mount Diablo.

Ransom's survey thus defined the division between private property and public land that would become the basis of Walker's association with the East Bay Regional Park District.

In turn, Mount Diablo became the center of Bob Walker's photographic world.

The foothills of Mount Diablo . . . Morgan Territory . . . Well, you know what they say about love at first sight. And to complicate matters, there was that friend who decided that my appreciation of the hills ought to be expressed with a camera, and sold me, almost gave me, his spare. If I had only known!

Bob Walker

Through Bob Walker's eyes, we cast our gaze eastward to the twin peaks of Mount Diablo and its foothills from the 6000 acre Briones Regional Park of the East Bay Regional Park District.

To our right as we face Mount Diablo, beyond the reach of Walker's camera, and beyond the Berkeley and Oakland Hills at our backs, stretches San Francisco Bay.

Directly behind us lies San Pablo Bay and to our distant left, the unseen Suisun Bay – the three bodies of water that outline the west and northern boundaries of the East Bay.

On the opposite side of Mount Diablo, inland and to the east, the landscape extends across the vast Sacramento-San Joaquin Delta and opens onto California's great Central Valley.

In the middle distance, beyond the green ridge carrying Briones Crest Trail (the crest itself is farther up the ridge off to our right), we can see the city of Walnut Creek along with parts of Concord and Pleasant Hill.

Within the landscape of the East Bay centered on Mount Diablo, this view perfectly illustrates the intertwined themes of city and countryside that form the heart and soul of Walker's photography.

A map on page 173 offers a comprehensive view of the entire region: Mount Diablo, San Francisco Bay, the East Bay, and the East Bay Regional Parks.

If you look closely on the map, you can even find the spot where Walker photographed this magnificent starting point for our exploration of his photography and the landscape that so captured his imagination.

Mount Diablo Vista

Mount Diablo
From Briones Regional Park
Northwest of Walnut Creek, California
December 1981

One of the most sublimely beautiful landscapes the world has to offer.

Bob Walker, speech at Contra Costa Conservation League Award Ceremony, 1991

One of Walker's favorite trees, a lone valley oak in Diablo Foothills Regional Park of the East Bay Regional Park District. It stands near an area once proposed as a freeway.

Sunset at Castle Rock

Diablo Foothills Regional Park
Southeast of Walnut Creek, California
February 1985

Behind lie the majestic battlements of Castle Rock. Today this solitary guardian watches over a continuous band of open space that connects the city of Walnut Creek's Walnut Creek Open Space with Mount Diablo State Park.

Soon after I first met Bob Walker, he asked if my wife and I had ever been to Morgan Territory, east of Mount Diablo. We had not, but the name alone sounded intriguing so off we went. Once past the town of Clayton, the houses thinned out then stopped altogether. Blue oaks and buckeyes began to define the landscape. Even the air was different. We rounded a corner and stopped in front of a For Sale sign tied to a rusty gate. Beyond the sign, an overgrown dirt road disappeared into a grove of trees.

Walker described how he had already talked to people at the East Bay Regional Park District about purchasing this particular patch of woodland, the Marshall property, as a park. According to Walker, the District still hadn't quite figured out what to do with the adjacent Morgan Territory parcels they had picked up several years earlier. Walker, of course, had seen the sign before, and waved us through the fence for our hike.

We didn't know it then, but we were among the first to experience what was to become Walker's modus operandi: take a few friends for a hike in an area already known to Walker, show them the beauty of the land, have them invite their friends – then do it again in an ever-widening circle. Finally, give everyone postcards to send to the East Bay Regional Park District declaring how important it was to save this particular patch of open space.

John Woodbury, General Manager, Parks and Open Space for Napa County

Walker's eye for color here focuses on extremely large examples of manzanita trees, the name taken from the Spanish for "little apple tree" – probably named for the shiny red berries that grow on the plant's twisting branches.

Marshall Property Manzanita

Morgan Territory Regional Preserve
North of Livermore, California
April 1984

The land where Walker took this image was acquired as an addition to Morgan Territory Regional Preserve by the East Bay Regional Park District in 1986.

Blue Oaks

Diablo Foothills Regional Park
Southeast of Walnut Creek, California
March 1991

Unlike the more solitary valley oaks, blue oaks – named for the bluish color of their leaves – often grow in clusters.

Seen here in Diablo Foothills Regional Park of the East Bay Regional Park District, a budding grove of thin, younger trees surrounds a mature elder. Long recognized for their ability to survive extremely harsh conditions, blue oaks have been known to decrease in height to conserve moisture during times of drought.

Little Pine Creek

Mount Diablo State Park
Southeast of Walnut Creek, California
March 1985

With little fresh inland surface water occurring naturally in the East Bay, Little Pine Creek offers a welcome oasis of light, sound, and movement on the slopes of Mount Diablo in Mount Diablo State Park.

Although fed by many nearby springs, including the upstream Coffeeberry Springs, Little Pine Creek flows only on a seasonal basis rather than year-round.

Ginochio Ranch

Private land below the ridgeline
Adjacent to Mount Diablo State Park
October 1984

Although many visitors to Mount Diablo State Park believe that the entire mountain is protected public open space, most of the rolling hills caught by Walker in this image belong to the Ginochio family.

Four generations of the Ginochios have grazed their cattle on 2000 acres of private land, one parcel viewed here below the dark hills of Black Point to the east. With ongoing pressures to convert farmland to housing developments, the fate of the Ginochio Ranch remains an open question.

The red tail hawk writes songs across the sky
There's music in the waters flowing by
And you can hear a song each time the wind sighs
In the golden rolling hills of California
In the golden rolling hills of California

It's been so long, love, since you said good-bye
My cabin's been as lonesome as a cry
But there's comfort in the wind song drifting by
In the golden, rolling hills of California
In the golden, rolling hills of California

George Schroder, the song *The Red Tail Hawk*, popularized by the singer Kate Wolf (1942–1986)

Golden Hills

Diablo Foothills Regional Park
East of Walnut Creek, California
May 1985

Although it may appear an eternal image of untouched, natural California countryside, this dry grassland with its mature valley oaks has been shaped and reshaped by human settlement.

For decades ranchers have grazed their cattle throughout the land of the East Bay. As a result, one sees virtually no undergrowth or seedlings on such hillsides as this, while the surviving valley oaks are all of a similar age.

Yet even with this knowledge of a profoundly altered landscape, the majestic natural sculpture of solitary oaks scattered across a golden backdrop continues to evoke the essence of open space in California.

In 1977, the East Bay Regional Park District in collaboration with the United States Bureau of Outdoor Recreation and the counties of Contra Costa, Alameda, and Santa Clara, produced a study of open space surrounding Mount Diablo.

Entitled "Diablo Ridgelands: A Multi-Jurisdictional Open Space Study," the research identified 850,000 acres as possible candidates for protection.

Although the political will did not exist at that time to advance such regional thinking, in effect "Diablo Ridgelands" became a blueprint for the future of the Park District.

Over time, Walker increasingly learned to use the moods and seasons of the East Bay to enhance his ability to convey the shape and dimensions of the landscape.

Time of day was critical. To capture the precise light that would define hills and ridgelines, Walker would wait for that special moment, always after 4:00 in the afternoon. Shadows would deepen and colors become infused with a rich intensity. Walker called this time "magic hour." His friends came to know it simply as "Bob's hour."

Changing seasons and equally, the changes that occur within each season likewise became crucial elements of Walker's photography. From observations made over the course of many years, Walker learned to take full advantage of the interaction between seasonal sunlight and the rolling hills of the East Bay.

Here, in the late afternoon, the rainy season draws to a close, south-facing slopes have already dried a light brown beneath the sun's direct glare. The more sheltered slopes facing north retain a breath of green. This combination of color and form allowed Walker to outline the contours of the receding hills with touches of gold.

By early autumn, the dry season ends and the grass bleaches dramatically to white, an elegant precursor to the green hills brought by winter's rain.

Since this image was made, the low-lying fields have been filled with houses, while the surrounding hills and ridges have been preserved within Sycamore Valley Regional Open Space Preserve.

Wood Ranch Afterglow

Sycamore Valley Regional Open Space Preserve
Danville, California
April 1989

Fallen Tree in Snow

Morgan Territory Regional Preserve
North of Livermore, California
February 1990

They say there are two seasons in California. Green in winter and brown in summer. If one were to ask Bob Walker, he might have replied that each day and every hour reveals a kaleidoscope of seasons if you take the time and care to look.

Sometimes the California seasons unfold over many years, as revealed by Walker's rare glimpse of a fallen tree outlined by a dusting of snow in Morgan Territory. Except for the gentle white cap that annually settles on Mount Diablo, such a snowfall comes only once or twice in a decade.

Mount Allison in Snow

Within Mission Peak Regional Preserve
East of Fremont, California
March 1985

As the landscape spreads outward from Mount Diablo, within 10 miles of downtown San Jose an "Arctic Express" blankets the hillsides and low-lying areas of Mount Allison with snow.

The peak, and its array of television broadcasting antennas, stands as private property within Mission Peak Regional Preserve. Mission Peak is the tallest of the three peaks in the area northeast of Mount Allison, with Monument Peak to the south.

Here, like a scene from the windswept Alaskan wilderness, Walker captures the virtually black-and-white beauty of a storm that began life in the far north and extended its global reach southward.

CHAPTER TWO

The Golden Gate and the East Bay

South Bay Sunset

Viewed from Mount Hamilton
East of Hayward, California
March 1985

The Golden Gate and the East Bay

Sloughs, salt ponds, and mudflats at the southernmost tip of San Francisco Bay, 50 miles from San Francisco and the Golden Gate to the north, characterize much of the bay's landscape. The hills in the distance mark the San Francisco Peninsula. Farther to the west, the low coastal mountains give way to farms, parks, and the rocky shoreline of the Pacific Ocean.

"San Francisco, open your Golden Gate," has long been a rallying cry in the region. The first inhabitants witnessed the Golden Gate before the rising waters of a warming planet flooded the valley that became San Francisco Bay. They found shelter and food by harvesting plants and animals along the shoreline.

Evidence of early human settlement remains in the form of "shellmounds" that surround the bay. Some believe these artificial hills comprised of mussel and oyster shells along with other animal remnants were sacred sites as revealed by the additional presence of human remains and ceremonial objects. Others see only more mundane signs of human activity in the form of discarded shells from simple meals.

Whatever their precise cultural significance, the historical heritage of the shellmounds remains an increasingly hidden secret in every corner of the shoreline, often covered by more recent urban development. Not far from the Bay Bridge and freeways that displaced so much of the original shoreline stood one of the larger mounds.

As tall as a four-story building and the length of a football field in diameter, the mound, on the original San Francisco Bay shoreline near Temescal Creek in Emeryville, was leveled and excavated beginning in the 1920s until finally covered over in 1999. Marked today by a small, parklike memorial, the mound lies beneath a shopping mall at the crossroad of Shellmound Street and Ohlone Way.

It took Europeans several attempts before they succeeded in entering San Francisco Bay. In 1542, the Portuguese explorer Juan Rodriguez Cabrillo sailed around South America's Cape Horn but missed the bay entirely before reaching Northern California's Russian River. Sir Francis Drake landed north of the bay in 1579, again without seeing or noting its existence.

Neither Sebastian Cermeño in 1595 nor Sebastian Vizcaíno in 1602 found the bay although both voyaged farther north along the coast. It was left to Gaspar de Portolá in 1769 to record the first European recognition of the bay's existence. Not until 1775 would Juan Ayala finally enter San Francisco Bay and direct his pilot, José de Cañizares, to map its shoreline.

In 1977, fresh out of college, Walker responded to the beckoning call of the Golden Gate. From Ohio he headed west and began to explore the new world of San Francisco Bay and later the East Bay counties of Contra Costa and Alameda, the area embraced by the East Bay Regional Park District.

Golden Gate Sunset

Seen from Albany, California
November 1987

The Golden Gate, seen from Albany on the "opposite coast" of Contra Costa County. From the south to our left the view sweeps across Yerba Buena Island (a natural island) and Treasure Island (artificial, constructed with landfill for the 1939 World's Fair) across San Francisco and the Golden Gate.

Continuing northward to the right, our view includes Angel Island (completely natural) which in turn conceals the onetime fishing village of Sausalito (mostly natural).

The silhouette of Angel Island blends visually with the dark heights of the Marin Headlands to the west (all natural except for the remnants of military outposts, a former Nike missile base, and Point Bonita Lighthouse), now protected as open space within the National Park system's Golden Gate National Recreation Area.

The tallest peak farther north is Mount Tamalpais (all natural with the exception of a few roads, communication towers, radar antennas plus an abandoned fire lookout on the summit), which oversees the bayside cities of Belvedere, Tiburon, Mill Valley, Corte Madera, Greenbrae, Larkspur, and San Rafael (all built since Mission San Rafael was constructed in 1817).

As Walker waited for his camera to tick off its time exposures, he would often try to picture in his mind's eye what the landscape looked like 150 or 200 years ago. A small stretch of the imagination easily erases the towers and bridges of the 21st century. What remains is a grand vista of tide and sky as it might have appeared to the first inhabitants and the European explorers who followed.

Temescal Creek Sunset

Eastshore State Park
West of Emeryville, California
October 1989

With the lights of San Francisco and the Bay Bridge as a backdrop, Temescal Creek in the Emeryville Crescent lies adjacent to an area once known for its free-form sculptures made of driftwood. The creek, one of the largest in the area, originates in the hills above Oakland. It descends into Lake Temescal, established as a regional park in 1936, then disappears into a culvert running beneath Highway 24.

But all is not lost. Thanks to a collaborative effort by the California Department of Parks and Recreation and the Coastal Conservancy with the leadership of the East Bay Regional Park District, Temescal eventually resurfaces. After twisting through an underground labyrinth, the creek emerges into the expanse of Emeryville Marsh, protected as part of Eastshore State Park, and completes its journey to San Francisco Bay.

With his painterly eye Walker captured the serpentine channel of Mowry Slough at the southern end of San Francisco Bay, part of the Don Edwards San Francisco Bay National Wildlife Refuge.

In the far distance stand the silhouetted peaks of the Santa Cruz Mountains, part of the Pacific Coast Range that looms above the Pacific Ocean from the town of Pacifica in the north to Santa Cruz on Monterey Bay to the south.

An important habitat for harbor seals, Mowry Slough runs alongside evaporating ponds used for salt production by the Cargill Corporation.

The salt ponds are the multicolored shapes glimpsed by travelers as they fly over the bay during landings at San Francisco International Airport. The green, red, and yellow colors come from different species of algae and brine shrimp that live in the varying salinities of individual ponds.

In 2001 Cargill agreed to sell 61 percent of its holdings to the United States Fish and Wildlife Service and California's Department of Fish and Game. Currently in full swing, the plan is to restore more than 15,000 acres of former salt ponds to tidal marsh and wildlife habitat.

The East Bay Park District will participate through the restoration of 600 acres of critical habitat and the creation of a new Eden Landing Ecological Reserve.

South Bay Slough

East of Fremont, California
North of San Jose, California
December 1987

33

San Francisco Bay is so large that often its storms are more disastrous to oceangoing craft than is the ocean itself in its violent moments. The waters of the bay contain all manner of fish, wherefore its surface is ploughed by the keels of all manner of fishing boats manned by all manner of fishermen.

Jack London, "White and Yellow," *Tales of the Fish Patrol* (1905)

As we look north from the southern tip of San Francisco Bay, our line of sight follows slough channels and former salt ponds in the Don Edwards San Francisco Bay National Wildlife Refuge toward the golden ridges of Coyote Hills Regional Park.

With the city of San Jose at our backs, the cities of Fremont, Union City, Hayward, San Leandro, and Oakland extend along the flat land to our right.

In the hills above the urban areas, a remarkable 25 miles of connected regional parks begins with Garin Regional Park to the immediate east and slightly north.

From there if we're feeling ambitious and our sense of grandeur has been awakened by the history that surrounds us, and by the scenic wonder of the parklands embraced by the East Bay Regional Park District, we would then set forth along the Bay Area Ridge Trail northward.

Within sight of our initial aerial vantage point, among several parks along the way, our stride would carry us through Anthony Chabot Regional Park with its family campgrounds, Redwood Regional Park known for its deeply forested trails, and the lava fields of Robert Sibley Volcanic Regional Preserve before reaching Tilden Regional Park above Berkeley.

A closer view – much closer, it should be noted – that shows one of the parks nestled among the others on our route, Huckleberry Botanic Regional Preserve, can be found on page 56.

As a crowning touch in Walker's soaring image, at the far upper right, a barely glimpsed Mount Diablo presides over the entire landscape from its lofty vantage point on the far side of the East Bay hills.

Slough with Coyote Hills in the Distance

Coyote Hills Regional Park
East of Newark, California
December 1987

spring rain
small shells on a small beach
glittering

    haiku poetry by Yosa Buson (1716–1783)

Storm Clouds

Between Oakland and Alameda, California
February 1986

Captured here in one small, intimate view, the western boundary of the East Bay Regional Park District runs along the eastern edge of San Francisco Bay from just above San Jose northward, past the cities of Oakland and San Francisco toward the Carquinez Strait. A regional map on page 173 offers a generalized overview.

Ground-level visits, however, offer more detailed and unexpected havens. San Francisco Bay appears less as a single body of water and more a series of smaller bays and inlets surrounded by marshlands, mudflats, and protected shorelines open to the public.

In Walker's glowing image of a passing storm, columns of sunlight fall through the cloud cover as we contemplate the sparkling expanse of San Leandro Bay from Martin Luther King, Jr. Regional Shoreline.

With its surprising picnic areas and recreational trails half-hidden alongside an industrial park, the Regional Shoreline also includes an important wildlife sanctuary, Arrowhead Marsh, off to our right.

Across San Leandro Bay, the city of Oakland extends a slender arm across the dark strip of land in the center. The Regional Shoreline continues to curl around the edge of the opposite shore while the treeline conceals Oakland International Airport at its back.

To the distant west, on the far side of an unseen San Francisco Bay, lie the hills of San Bruno Mountain and the city of South San Francisco with San Francisco International Airport at their feet.

Thunderhead at Sunset

Over San Francisco Bay
Near Hayward Regional Shoreline
West of Hayward, California
March 1987

A rare San Francisco Bay thunderstorm fills the sky like a churning ocean wave in this image taken by Walker from the Hayward Regional Shoreline.

Beneath the waters of the bay, visible at low tide from a trail along the shoreline, visitors can see the decaying wooden pilings of shipping docks. The all-but-vanished piers were built in the 1850s to deliver wheat by boat to San Francisco.

Hayward Regional Shoreline is extremely important because it marks the beginnings of salt pond restoration on the Bay. The first project at Cogswell Marsh was completed in 1980.

This initial success pointed the way to large-scale restoration efforts now underway in the South Bay and alongside Highway 37 at the northern tip of San Pablo Bay.

CHAPTER THREE

The Beauty

The Oaks

Slopes of Flag Hill
Sunol Regional Wilderness
Southeast of Sunol, California
April 1987

The Beauty

And then there's the sheer beauty of the place.

From the time of Walker's first encounter with the East Bay, it immediately captured his imagination, and, one would have to say, his heart.

Why this landscape resonated so strongly with Walker remains something of a mystery. Walker also spent time a fair amount of time camping in the Grand Canyon and Sierra Nevada as well as photographing their craggy peaks and canyons, storm-laden skies, and lingering sunsets.

Although Walker wrote many articles and letters on conservation issues during his lifetime, his interior thoughts about the particular affection he held for the East Bay are far fewer. The handful of personal notebooks he left behind offer a handful of rough drafts for his public presentations and lists of daily tasks to be accomplished.

Part of the reason the East Bay drew Walker's attention was certainly its proximity to Walker's home in San Francisco. Most of the Bay's parks and open countryside could be reached via BART and a bus ride or two. Compared to an expensive, time-consuming drive by automobile or lengthy ride by bus to the Sierra Nevada, to say nothing of the Grand Canyon, the East Bay was in Walker's own backyard.

Add to this the East Bay Regional Park District's policy toward dogs, meaning that they were not only accepted but welcomed to most parks – at long last, the guy looking for a place to walk his dog had found nirvana.

Ease of access, though, was only part of it. During Walker's slide-shows he often spoke about his appreciation for the intertwining and blending of city and countryside that makes San Francisco Bay and the East Bay region so remarkable.

There was, however, more to it even than that. There was something comforting about the scale of the East Bay and on certain days, at certain moments, qualities Walker found magical.

Through his photography, Walker began to express his emotional responses to the East Bay: by turns depicting the landscape in contrast between the easily seen and the half-hidden: a veritable fireworks of wildflowers photographed on one day and the same location veiled by shadow and fog or snow on another.

From his written words and from the recollections of friends, in the end it's not difficult to imagine how Walker would have summarized his response to questions about his affection for the East Bay. It was simple, he might have said, obvious in fact – all you had to do was take a look.

A fantastic area in its own right and where wild life exists so close to us, so very close to our communities, and really makes for that experience of the Bay Area of both wild and the city that I think is so very special.

Bob Walker, Pleasanton Ridge slideshow, 1988

Deer on Ridgetop

Lime Ridge Open Space
Owned by the cities of Walnut Creek
    and Concord, California
Viewed with the city of Walnut Creek behind
December 1986

Walker often commented how rare it was to make even one photograph that began to equal what he felt outdoors on even the most ordinary day, the often surprising emotional and visual layers of the experience.

Beneath shading trees atop slender Lime Ridge, within sight of an urban area, Walker achieved his goal of finding one such photograph. One can almost feel the light breeze cresting the ridge with its rustle of leaf and grass as Walker approached a favorite viewpoint overlooking Walnut Creek.

In this setting of open space intermingled with city, Walker encountered and photographed one of the East Bay's small wonders, a group of black-tailed deer. Perhaps it's more accurate judging from their curious and attentive stance to say that the deer, called *mule deer* by some, encountered Walker.

Pieced together over the course of 20 years, Lime Ridge Open Space exemplifies a growing spirit of intergovernmental and citizen cooperation throughout the East Bay.

With partial funding and assistance from the East Bay Regional Park District, this oasis of open space was created by the cities of Walnut Creek and Concord in cooperation with the citizen advocacy groups Save Mount Diablo and the Walnut Creek Open Space Foundation.

For you who climb to the top of Mission Peak, don't just walk over the land to see the view. Walk through the land, understand the history, become part of it. Drink in the beauty and let the peace envelope you in its arms of enduring strength. If done this way, you may exert yourself, mentally in the learning and physically in getting to the top, but your abilities will have been strengthened far more than you realize : physically, mentally and emotionally.

Roan McClure, "Mission Peak: Silent Southbay Sentinel, "Omega Foundation website

This landscape by Walker with its small group of wild goats on the lower slopes of Mission Peak bears witness to the not atypical evolution of a regional park, in this case Mission Peak Regional Preserve.

In 1978, the Park District purchased Peak Meadow Ranch (est. 1928) from the McClure family, the land pictured in Walker's sunset-bathed image. Minnis Ranch, which included nearby Monument Peak, was added that same year. A third ranch, Wool Ranch, which contains most of adjacent Mount Allison, was acquired much later, in 1988.

The three peaks, Mission Peak, Mount Allison, and Monument Peak, together form Mission Ridge running north to south, all now within the limits of the Preserve. A wintery view of Mount Allison cloaked beneath a lace of snow can be found on page 23.

In 2005, to honor the 114th anniversary of Margaret Moore McClure's birth, the McClure family formally expressed their thanks in writing to the Park District. They praised the concern and effort "that your staff has taken in the on-going care and costly preservation over 24 years of Peak Meadow Ranch."

Wild Goats Below Mission Peak

Mission Peak Regional Preserve
Southeast of Fremont, California
November 1984

Later acquisitions to the Preserve restored an open-space corridor that links the Mission Peak Regional Preserve in Alameda County with Ed R. Levin County Park in Santa Clara County.

Stories vary about the wild goats. Perhaps their ancestors escaped from a farm.

Margaret McClure remembered purposely releasing a pair in the 1930s. She called them Pyramis and Thisbe after the doomed "Romeo and Juliet" lovers in the epic poem, "Metamorphoses," by the Roman poet, Ovid.

In 1965, Margaret's grandson, Roan McClure, and Julie Goodale, a family friend, released a second pair named George and Gwen after Julie's parents.

Other rumors and stories claim the goats were released to provide sport for hunters. If so, they may have turned the tables. A few goats seem to have survived on the flanks of Mission Peak, while the hunters have long since departed.

Here winter and spring bring water to the dry hills. Low-lying land offers a fertile cradle for water-loving plants. Blue-eyed grass and ever-present yellow gold-fields spread across the lush meadow like a carpet.

This quiet refuge was one of Walker's favorite places to visit – close enough to reach from his Haight-Ashbury apartment in San Francisco after an easy drive and a modest hike; far enough to enter another, more peaceful world.

Spring Campsite

Morgan Territory Regional Preserve
North of Livermore, California
April 1988

49

Morgan Territory Poppies

Morgan Territory Regional Preserve
North of Livermore, California
March 1991

As much as Walker appreciated and made a great deal of effort to capture the details of the land he cherished, he often joked how little he knew about the names of plants and animals.

The land is covered, he once said, with three kinds of plants: flowers, trees, and everything else. When pressed for specifics, he occasionally acknowledged the existence of a fourth category, bushes.

Yet his love for wildflowers was boundless. Walker always maintained a lovely urban garden in the backyard of his San Francisco apartment.

Whether or not he knew more about the names and lore of flowers than he let on, in the smallest blossom Walker saw an infinity of detail as great as that found in any of his most sweeping and vibrant landscapes.

California "Golden" Poppies

Eschscholzia californica
Morgan Territory Regional Preserve
East of Livermore, California
April 1989

Named the state flower of California in 1903, the California poppy has been a favorite topic of poets since the Gold Rush of 1849.

Among them, Joaquin Miller (1837–1913), for whom beautiful, redwood-cloaked Joaquin Miller Regional Park in the Oakland Hills was named, wrote:

> The golden poppy is Gold's gold,
> The gold that lifts nor weighs us down,
> The gold that knows no miser's hold,
> The gold that banks not in the town,
> But singing, laughing, freely spills
> Its hoard far up the happy hills;
> Far up, far down, at every turn –
> What beggar has not gold to burn!

A self-styled free-spirit, Miller – born Cincinnatus Hiner Miller – created his pen name after the legendary California outlaw and folk hero Joaquin Murieta.

Visitors today can still walk through "The Abby," a surviving remnant of Miller's home in the Oakland Hills, called *The Hights* in Miller's eccentric spelling.

This historic landmark where Miller lived from 1886 until his death, offers a taste of an early bohemian hailed in his lifetime as the "Poet of the Sierra" and "California's Own."

53

There is perhaps no nature-study that can yield the same amount of pure and unalloyed pleasure with so little outlay as the study of the wild flowers. When one is interested in them, every walk into the fields is transformed from an aimless ramble into a joyous, eager quest, and every journey upon stage or railroad becomes a rare opportunity for making new plant-acquaintances – a season of exhilarating excitement.

Mary Elizabeth Parsons, *The Wild Flowers of California, Their Names, Haunts, and Habits* (1897)

Baby Blue-Eyes

Nemophila menziesii
Ohlone Wilderness Regional Preserve
East of Sunol, California
April 1987

The delicate, delicate, exquisite blossoms of baby blue-eyes – described by Elizabeth Parsons from her home in San Rafael, California so many years ago, it seems as though her words cannot possibly apply to our era of automobiles and instant technological communication:

> When skies are smiling and the earth is already clothed with a luxuriant and tender herbage, we find upon some balmy morning that the baby blue-eyes have opened in gentle surprise upon the lovely world.

Parsons' words remind us that although their petals perish with the first frost of autumn, each year in a seemingly eternal pattern, the blossoms of baby blue-eyes open once again, to greet the lengthening days of spring.

Jumbo Jym Mushroom

Gymnopilus sp.
Huckleberry Botanic Regional Preserve
East of and adjacent to Oakland, California
c. 1987, early spring

Clinging to a statuesque moss-furred oak, Jumbo Jym, one member of a remnant plant community found nowhere else in the East Bay, flourishes in a preserve noted for its fog-enhanced climate and rich soil.

Walker's image reveals a thick layer of fallen leaves that contribute to that richness.

The damp, dense ground cover bears witness to the area's long-term resistance to large-scale forest fires that would otherwise have cleared the forest floor.

Huckleberry Preserve is but one jewel in a remarkable chain of parks that line the hills above the heavily urbanized shoreline cities to the west.

The parks range southward from slender Wildcat Canyon Regional Park in the north to include Tilden Regional Park, Claremont Canyon Regional Preserve, and Robert Sibley Volcanic Regional Preserve before reaching Huckleberry.

A wider vista looking up toward these parks from San Francisco Bay appears on page 35.

From Huckleberry, the ridgeline parks continue southward until they reach a concluding crescendo with Redwood Regional Park and Anthony Chabot Regional Park.

The great variety of hill and valley, forest and plain, the absence of winter cold or summer heat, and the easy accessibility from all parts of the urban area, bring to the fortunate people of the East Bay cities a continuous opportunity for the enjoyment of the great outdoors, under the most favorable conditions . . . The most beautiful combination of mountain and marine scenery that America affords.

Frederick Law Olmsted and Ansel F. Hall, *Proposed Park Reservations for East Bay Cities* (1930)

Tilden Falls below Lake Anza

Tilden Regional Park
Adjacent to Berkeley, California
February 1986

Below Lake Anza, in Tilden Regional Park, a shaded fall of water removes visitors from the sights and sounds of adjacent Berkeley's hustle and bustle. Along with Lake Temescal Regional Park and Robert Sibley Volcanic Regional Preserve, Tilden was created in 1934 as one of the Park District's first three parks.

It's always a pleasure to play Tilden – the most beautiful golf course anywhere in the Bay Area – but it can be a humbling experience.

Sam Shannon, Ambassador, Tilden Park Golf Course

Tilden, Pond Reflections

Tilden Regional Park
Adjacent to Berkeley, California
March 1986

Looking across a reflecting pond to the putting green on the par 4 third hole at Tilden Park Golf Course. For people who love golf, Tilden holds a special place.

Devilishly challenging and exquisitely beautiful due to the steep elevations and surrounding redwoods of the course, Tilden recalls an earlier era with its truly vintage twists, turns, and dips, designed in 1933 by a legendary golf course architect, William Park Bell.

Not a golfer himself, Walker's mirrored landscape nevertheless seems to echo the tranquility and concentration honored by golfers as the inner game, all cloaked in the filtered sunlight of a coastal forest.

From a distance as I walked uphill toward that cluster of rocks on the ridgetop, I'd be looking for the larger birds, the predators: the kestrel, red-tailed hawk, the prairie falcon; then as I walked closer I'd keep my eyes open for the phoebe and the rock wren. This kind of island of rock is the perfect place to find rock wrens. Just perfect.

Tom Steller, Head Curator, Natural Sciences Department, Oakland Museum of California

Storm over Del Valle Canyon

Seen from Ohlone Wilderness
East of Sunol, California
February 1987

Hiking with friends on a ridgetop not too far from this rock outcrop in the Ohlone Wilderness, Walker stopped to photograph the landscape. Ominous clouds began to fill the sky. The temperature plunged. Heavy drops of rain began to snap and pop against the light jackets of the hapless hikers.

With a deep and unanimous sigh, the group reversed direction and began a grudging retreat toward the head of the trail.

Well, not quite unanimous. Walker shoved his camera into his ever-present belt pack and headed for the shelter of the nearest tree. "Where's everyone going?" he called, "I'm staying for rainbows."

Another form of rocky outcropping, this one made by human hands. Seen in various locations throughout the East Bay and the regional parks, the walls have defied historical analysis.

No one can say exactly who built them or when, not even historians or anthropologists from one of the many universities in the East Bay.

Some say the walls were built by Chinese laborers after they finished building the transcontinental railroad. Others say an Amish family built at least one set of walls as they cleared the land in preparation for farming.

Yet the land surrounding the walls has never felt the cut of the plow for farming. The hillsides have historically been used only for grazing cattle. Rocks would never have been an issue.

One wonders why else you would bother clearing the land. Perhaps in hopes of containing the cattle. On the other hand, many of the walls are too low to stop a determined grazing animal, neither cattle nor deer.

For whatever reason they were built or whatever purpose they served, the walls remind us how little we sometimes know about our own backyards.

In an age where science seems to have all the answers, we have encountered yet one more mystery of the East Bay.

Rock Wall with Farm Road

East of Mission Peak Regional Preserve
February 1985

I've really felt evangelical about making people stop and realize that they're in the middle of a very stunning landscape. It's all around them, and so accessible, but often they've overlooked it because California is loaded with so many superlatives.

Bob Walker, *Diablo Magazine*, December 1992

When many people first encounter a Bob Walker photograph, like this view of a natural rock formation named after the Great Wall of China, they often do a double-take. After being told the location of the image, they almost can't believe it's from the East Bay . . . or that they've never seen it before . . . or even heard of it.

Thereby stands revealed one of the main lessons of Walker's life and photography: you have to get out there on the land itself to experience the full wonder of the East Bay.

Lesson number two: more times than you might think, you can never quite imagine what you'll find, no matter which guide books you read or websites you visit – like a great wall of rock plunked down in the middle of a hillside in Diablo Foothills Regional Park.

China Wall

Diablo Foothills Regional Park
January 1985

Dark Trees at Sunset

Diablo Foothills Regional Park
East of Walnut Creek, California
January 1985

Although an avid writer of letters and articles to support his vision of land conservation, Walker wrote few introspective words about the artistic meaning and intent of his photographs. Nor did he record technical information on his photography while taking his pictures.

Beyond giving titles to his favorite images for purposes of exhibition, Walker would occasionally write detailed location notes directly on his slide mounts.

Dates of the pictures' taking would be recorded by the automatic numbers stamped on the thin cardboard sleeves holding the original slides after their processing.

Sometimes, as in this image reminiscent of a romantic landscape painting from the 19th century, mood replaces title, caption, even location. The landscape with its half-barren tree leaves the viewer alone with private thoughts at the close of another day.

We would often camp with Bob in this favorite place of ours that felt very remote. A different world. Even the name was exotic, a territory. An unchanged land. Yet deeply connected with people.

Below our campsite were grinding rocks used by Native Americans for thousands of years to grind acorns for their food supply. I'd often go for early morning walks to follow in their footsteps and take in the sense of peace we found in Morgan Territory.

John Woodbury, the hiker in the fog, General Manager, Parks and Open Space for Napa County

Hiker in Fog

Morgan Territory Regional Preserve
North of Livermore, California
December 1981

Silence. Stillness. No cars, no phones. No TV sets, no glowing screens. Walker's moody portrait of a hiker in the fog offers a reminder that some of the most important experiences of the East Bay Regional Park District are interior.

In its own way each park provides boundless opportunities to be apart, to reflect, find room for the imagination to recharge and expand, the body to relax – places where an inner quiet blends with the breath of wind and the caress of fog.

The only thing was the mines. Just dig coal. It was hard work. Hard to make a living. It was tough. Yeah, it was tough work. They had to lay on their stomachs 'cause every vein would be just so wide. They wouldn't dig the rest of it. And then they'd have to take and put timber in there. Board it up so it wouldn't cave in or nothin'. My dad'd come home from work, "Go get me some beer." Give us a quarter. We walked about a mile and got the beer.
John Buffo (1893–1987), *Black Diamond Oral History Project*, East Bay Regional Park District

Tule Fog Shrouds the Hills

Black Diamond Mines Regional Preserve
South of Pittsburg and Antioch, California
December 1982

From the 1860s into the beginning of the 20th century, Black Diamond coal mines, now the Black Diamond Mines Regional Preserve of the East Bay Regional Park District, stood forth as a major source of energy throughout the state of California.

Nearly 4 million tons of low-quality "lignite" coal were excavated to fuel a growing energy demand for transportation, manufacturing, and home heating.

As larger coal mines developed in Washington State and as oil become a more prominent source of energy, the coal mines of Black Diamond were abandoned. The surface land above the mines was given over to farmland for grazing cattle.

Some believe cattle then traced orderly contour lines called *terracettes* around the steep, rounded hills during their daily migration in search of food.

Others are less certain. Perhaps subsurface movement alone, they say, or some kind of land subsidence in combination with grazing cattle produced the evenly-spaced lines. No one really knows for sure.

Whatever their cause, Walker highlighted the terracettes' subtle sense of order while acknowledging their mystery in an otherwise silent, fog-enshrouded landscape.

It breaks our heart, is hard to part
With one who was so kind
Where shall we go to ease our woe
Or soothe our troubled minds?

Headstone of Sarah Norton (d. 1879), inscribed by her son

Rose Hill Cemetery

Black Diamond Mines Regional Preserve
South of Pittsburg and Antioch, California
January 1983

Many Welsh and Irish names are etched into these headstones on a hill above the ghost town of Somersville, the final resting place for miners and their families who came to America in search of a better life.

In addition to the daily hazards faced by the coal miners, epidemics of diptheria and untimely deaths during childbirth added to the travail of the mining families.

A white graveside marker captured by Walker on a fog-swept afternoon reveals the hopes and dreams of one such family. The inscription has been worn down by the patient work of time and the elements, as worn down as the immigrants were by the harsh life that greeted their arrival.

In the white stone of the Jenkins' plot, it's possible to learn the fate that greeted the family's arrival in America and their new home in the coal fields of the East Bay.

The names and dates on the marker in Walker's image read: "Thomas Joseph, Mar 2, 1869 – Aug 5, 1870; Elizabeth Ann, Aug 2, 1870 – Sept 22, 1870; Ebenezer, Dec 4, 1866 – June 23, 1874"; and finally the boy whose name suggests the family's longing for a second chance: a second Thomas Joseph, whose life lasted from July 30, 1872, to September 5, 1877.

A quarter moon rises above a silhouetted ridgetop in Black Diamond Mines Regional Preserve, one of the most accessible locations in the Park District, a 10-minute drive up a winding canyon along Somersville Road where it diverges from Highway 4 near Antioch.

Within minutes after arrival, visitors are transported to another time and place. A short uphill walk to the nearby ghost town of Somersville becomes a journey into the past.

Although no structures remain, visitors can stand on the levelled site of Somersville's vanished homes a short distance below Rose Hill Cemetery.

As one gazes at mine tailings across the narrow valley, the past beckons. Thoughts begin to conjure what the bustling town of Somersville and its siblings, Nortonville, Somersville, West Hartley, and Judsonville, might have looked like when mining was in full swing.

From the 1840s until about 1900, 4 million tons of coal were mined by hand from more than 200 miles of underground tunnels.

One can almost hear the sounds of clanking machinery, the scuffle of dark-clad miners in their heavy clothing, and the hearty Welsh and Irish accents of the immigrants who came to work the seams of coal.

A second wave of excavation from the 1920s until 1949 produced 1.8 million tons of powdery high-grade sand for the production of glass. That antique milk bottle or Depression-era glass that's been floating around the family for years might have originated as sand from one of the Black Diamond mines.

It's even possible to get a more direct and immediate physical impression of what it was like to work in the mines during Somersville's heyday. The East Bay Regional Park District offers guided tours 400 feet underground into the abandoned Hazel-Atlas Mine.

Visitors encounter dimly-lit passageways, the iron rails that carried mining cars laden with coal, the mine manager's underground office, and the weighty sense of pressing earth above one's head.

From either perspective, looking down at the abandoned mine or emerging from its narrow confines, it's a relief to stand free and clear in the open air and ascend the surrounding hills.

There you may discover yourself retracing the footsteps of Bob Walker. In every direction hikers will be greeted by one of his images, none more spectacular or special than Walker's view of a darkened ridge, as a ghostly curl of fog gathers in a hollow of the surrounding hills.

Black Diamond Moonrise

Black Diamond Mines Regional Preserve
South of Pittsburg and Antioch, California
November 1981

77

CHAPTER FOUR

The Mosaic

Windmill and Water Tank

Private land in the Tassajara Hills
Along Camino Tassajara Road
Near Danville, California
October 1985

The Mosaic

For a time during the 1940s and into the 1960s, all the pieces of life in the East Bay seemed to fit together. Like one of the modern art mosaics of the era, each individual piece had its place in creating a cohesive regional portrait.

Rural countryside seemed distinct from urban life, small regional cities like Pleasanton, Walnut Creek, and Brentwood had their own character, separated from one another, and all were a good distance from the region's major cities.

Press agents and writers neatly divided California into twelve basic regions. They gave them colorful names: the Redwood Empire, Gold Country, the Inland Empire. The impressive names described respectively, the northern coast up through Humboldt and Fort Bragg, the foothills of the Sierra Nevada east of Sacramento toward Sonora, and the southern lands east of Los Angeles from Riverside and San Bernardino across the Imperial Valley into the Sonoran Desert.

One image of the good life was encapsulated in the era's concept of town-and-country shopping centers, with little awareness that the shingled concentration of shops and covered walkways would become precursors to malls and superstores.

The supreme symbol and reality that linked these disparate regions was the open road.

Traffic might slow to a stately pace during rush hour, but traffic jams were virtually nonexistent. That was something you'd expect in the land of smog and urban sprawl in the southern part of the state, but not here. Not in the well-tempered mosaic of the East Bay.

Here in the north, automobiles whisked wide-eyed children and supposedly content adults across miles of scenic two-lane blacktop. The Bayshore Highway skirted the East Bay from north to south running right next to the bay. San Francisco was known as The City, with Oakland a close second, and pretty much everything else in-between was either small towns or countryside.

In 1956, one milk distribution company took advantage of the town-and-country concept to coin a commercial slogan, "Farms in Berkeley?" And the answer? What else? "Moooo." Even if there weren't really dairy farms in the town of Berkeley, they did exist throughout the farmlands of the East Bay, in the counties of Contra Costa and Alameda.

The mosaic of farm, small town, and undeveloped countryside seemed as fixed in time and place as did the survey lines that swept from the summit of Mount Diablo. An orderly and prosperous array of open space, small towns, and regional cities. What a thought. It seemed almost too good to be true.

North of Highway 580, north of Livermore, the trees and golden fields of alfalfa in Walker's image, along with so many others in the surrounding hills, have since been removed to clear the way for suburban housing.

The flowing contours of the hills beyond the large tree in the center were levelled to make way for a ridgetop golf course.

Several years after Walker's death, three photographers revisited the roadside where Walker took this gentle photograph to record the altered landscape.

Bulldozers roared in every direction. Earth movers scraped topsoil from alongside the old two-lane road and used it to fill the low lying depression at the base of the hillside. The rusted barbed wire fences were mostly collapsed and shoved aside. The crops, of course, were long gone.

It was hard to figure out where Walker had stood to make his original picture.

One of the group approached a nearby construction supervisor leaning on his white pick-up to ask for help. Where was the tree Walker placed at the center of his photograph?

The supervisor looked up from his clipboard, "That's all gone; I think it's over there with the rest of the stuff," and pointed to a pile of twisted wire fence and broken branches.

Hayfield, Fallon Road

North of Pleasanton, California
May 1985

Dougherty Valley

East of San Ramon, California
April 1989

One of the largest housing developments in the state of California with 12,000 homes now stand in a landscape where distant cattle grazed.

The diagonal stripes in the foreground reveal where windrows of hay had been allowed to dry in the field after the spring harvest. The hay was then gathered into hay bales before being removed and stacked to feed cattle during the following winter.

As the Dougherty development progressed, its ridges and valleys were not so much landscaped as eliminated, the ridgetops scoured for topsoil to fill the low-lying valley.

Las Positas Hills

North of Livermore, California
February 1987

For Sale signs and subdivided ranchettes with huge homes now stand not far from the spot where Walker originally took his exquisitely balanced and serene photograph.

To some, the hills along Morgan Territory Road are poised to accept the expanding population of Livermore. Others envision their continued use for ranching or their future preservation as public open space.

Hayfields and Rolling Hills

Private Land
Near Livermore, California
April 1986

In an area known as the Fertile Crescent, agricultural open space is here represented by rows of cut alfalfa grown for use as livestock feed.

While still maintained as agricultural land, the crops of today are more likely to be grapes for wine production than feed for cattle.

89

Tassajara Windrows

Danville, California
June 1986

Along Camino Tassajara Road, south of the Blackhawk housing development, stretched the low-lying farmland of the Wendt Ranch. When photographed by Walker, the alfalfa crop had been raked into windrows and left on the ground to dry prior to being baled for cattle feed.

Nothing of this landscape remains save the slender thread of Alamo Creek marked by the few trees at the edge of the field. The hills behind have been removed, their soil used to create flat pads for new homes.

Farm at Sunset

Private land
North of Pleasanton, California
March 1990

This farm, on Fallon Road in the Tassajara Hills north of Highway 580, was once typical of the agricultural land throughout the East Bay.

The rough-hewn wooden buildings stand increasingly isolated in an area giving way to housing developments, industrial parks, and a nearby community college.

A two-lane blacktop that led to the farm has become a one-way frontage road that feeds into a manicured four-lane boulevard serving a partially gated housing development.

CHAPTER FIVE

The Onslaught

This has the interesting face here where they actually provided me with a before-and-after sense of the changes that can come to a landscape when development moves up into the ridges. We need to look not only at what's been happening locally but realize cumulatively what we're in for in the next 10 years.

Mount Diablo Before and After

Former Blackhawk Ranch
Danville, California
February 1987

The Onslaught

Starting in the 1970s, it wasn't so much the fact that the East Bay faced an upsurge in new housing. From the beginning people had built their homes on the land. They had always transformed the landscape as they went. The transformation may have been pushing down tall grass and gathering it for reed homes or turning grasslands under for fields and barns.

Gathering momentum throughout the 1980s, anyone who lived in the Bay area had to be impressed – or dismayed – by the speed and size of the new construction.

Forget the old architectural wisdom taught in college, "form follows function" and "blend with the environment," this was the assembly-line pure and simple, the manufacturing of an entirely new landscape, one more conducive to mass construction, and mass marketing.

Walker witnessed the onslaught from the perspective of the land he'd grown to love. Entire hillsides removed, rolling hills leveled. No wonder he joked about the image he called "Matchstick Houses" (page 101) saying that the structures had been dropped by space aliens during the night while America slept.

Walker once told the story of driving home on Highway 580 past Pleasanton on the way back to San Francisco after a day photographing the eastern slopes of Mount Diablo. Suddenly he became disoriented; red taillights flared on every side. The entire freeway on which he was driving had been relocated between the time he left San Francisco and the time he drove back.

In time Walker recorded an almost unprecedented restructuring of the East Bay, a process increasingly taking place throughout California, the United States, and across the world. As few others have done, Walker understood that it was important to document the land before, during, and after the transformation. Otherwise, it would be almost impossible to imagine that so much land had changed so quickly.

One of Walker's most significant photographs. Very few shots exist that show us what we lost when they built Los Vaqueros reservoir: the farms, the valley oaks, the people who lived there, Ordway Ranch, Kellogg Creek, all long gone.

A very significant historical photograph that's going to be even more significant in the future, because the debate's already begun on making both Los Vaqueros Reservoir and Shasta Dam up north larger than they already are.

Bob Doyle, Assistant General Manager for Land Acquisitions, East Bay Regional Park District

Cañada de Los Vaqueros

South of Brentwood, California
January 1986

Here in what was once called Rancho Cañada de Los Vaqueros, or Ranch in the Canyon of the Cowboys, Walker uses seasonal color variations in adjoining crops and grasses to outline the twisting course of a small creek.

This stretch of fertile farmland along Vasco Road, where rodeos were once held dating back to the early 19th century days of the Spanish land grants, now lies beneath the surface of Los Vaqueros Reservoir.

The issues raised by the completion of Los Vaqueros Reservoir in 1998 are far from resolved. Plans now being considered by Contra Costa Water District would increase the dam's capacity by nearly five times and cover even more of the surrounding countryside.

The fundamental dilemma we face is balancing the needs of our natural systems and lands with the impulse to convert that bounty for short term economic gain.

Bob Walker

Matchstick Houses

Danville, California
March 1989

The ridges behind the new construction have since been protected by the city of Danville and the East Bay Regional Park District as a required "condition to permit development."

The negotiated and, in the end, cooperative approach of all parties involved, including the housing developers, established the Sycamore Valley Open Space, a 350-acre jewel of ridgetop preservation.

Canyon Lakes, "The Lake"

Sycamore Valley
With Coyote Creek beyond
Canyon Lakes Subdivision
February 1987

An artificial lake in an artificial landscape destined to receive 3100 new homes.

"Unfolding is a vast, majestic, enchanting kingdom cradled between the fabled Mount Diablo foothills and the golden San Ramon Valley. . . in scope and style, may well be the most exciting and historic master-planned community of the decade . . . a world specially tuned to the unique lifestyles and tastes that would emerge through the new millennium and beyond . . . perhaps the fastest growing, most affluent suburban and executive commercial center in the nation."

— Developer's website for Canyon Lakes

After the artificial lake has been landscaped, it's time to add the lakeside homes.

"Elaborate neighborhood guard gates, grand stone walls, elegant wrought iron fences provide the utmost security and privacy. Each neighborhood setting was designed to take advantage of the fabulous views, assuring that each home, no matter its size and location, would enjoy spectacular vistas of hillsides, lakes, or fairways."

— Developer's website for Canyon Lakes, conclusion

Canyon Lakes Construction

San Ramon, California
February 1987

The "Kibbutz"

Canyon Lakes subdivision
San Ramon, California
August 1987

"The first houses have already begun to circle themselves around the swimming pool for protection against the threatening hills."

— Bob Walker slideshow

As we look at the potential for change, we need to look at the larger picture, the beauty of the Bay Area, the balance between having wonderful cities and all the attractions within and the open ridgelands so close at hand. If we simply go through with plans that are currently contemplated, we may very well end up like those areas in the Bay Area that have seen most of their open space vanish. Perhaps within 10 years time, there will be no more open ridgelands.

Bob Walker, slideshow, 1988

Blackhawk Circle

San Ramon, California
February 1987

Southwest of Mount Diablo, in the former Blackhawk Ranch, dozens of new homes would eventually be constructed on the circular hill in the middle. Deer Hollow Drive loops to the right while Deer Ridge Drive circles to the left.

In a settlement negotiated by Save Mount Diablo, the rolling hills in the upper right were donated to Mount Diablo State Park by the developer to compensate for the loss of open space – the single largest donation of land made to the California State Park system since its inception in 1927.

The walnut groves of Walnut Creek are all but gone. The orchards of Bishop Ranch have been replaced by more tidy corporate landscapes. With the valleys all but gone, our beloved hills now feel the onslaught of the bulldozer, and building pads replace the irreplaceable grandeur of our ridges.

Bob Walker, speech, Contra Costa Conservation League Award Ceremony, 1991

Walker believed that if the ridges could be kept free of housing developments, then people living in the urban and suburban areas below would always have a visual open space available to them – no matter whether they were rich or poor.

In Walker's aerial photograph, the rolling hills of the ridgelands have been bulldozed to provide level pads for new housing. Concrete "drainage benches," the ribbed areas carefully lining low points in the hills, have been constructed to mimic the anti-erosion characteristics of grasses, plants, shrubs, and trees.

Ridgetop Development

Dublin, California
April 1986

We've made great strides: vast systems of preserved open space, and laws to protect our air, water, and wetlands. But the losses are cumulative, and the effects, increasingly devastating. . . . The challenge facing us is clearly great, the odds, no better.

Bob Walker, speech, Contra Costa Conservation League Award Ceremony, 1991

Construction Site, The Arrow

Crow Canyon at Camino Tassajara
San Ramon, California
February 1987

As Walker continued to witness the onslaught, and even then not often, his photographs took a darker turn, this particular image among them. With its overcast sky and twisted dead-end sign knocked off-center by unseen forces, the image seems to ask, where do we go from here?

The moment that someone is driving down the road and suddenly sees a bulldozer or some grading or a house under construction high in the hills where they never imagined development would take place is the moment they individually cross the line and say to themselves, "This has to be stopped."

Bob Walker, *Contra Costa Times*, August 27, 1990

In what can be interpreted as a form of self-portrait, the photographer's car acts as a stand-in for Walker himself. It waits beneath storm-heavy skies in the slanting light of a late afternoon as if it had an appointment to keep.

Carolyn Rissanen of the Natural Sciences Department of the Oakland Museum of California (the permanent home of the Bob Walker Photography Collection) noted that it's possible to trace Walker's footsteps from his car to the low hill where he took this photograph.

It's as if Walker were saying in picture form that none of us, including Walker himself, can be excluded from responsibility for the transformation of the world around us.

In our automobiles, in the patterns of our life, Walker might have been saying, we are all equally part of the problem and part of the solution.

Subdivision with Red Car

Canyon Lakes subdivision
San Ramon, California
February 1987

CHAPTER SIX

Activism and Achievement

The House on the Ridge

Pleasanton Ridge
Now Pleasanton Ridge Regional Park
West of Pleasanton, California
March 1986

Activism and Achievement

For Walker and others who shared his concern with the onslaught of massive suburban development, the 1980s became a time of struggle and despair, triumph and hope. The onslaught intensified and Walker became more directly involved with attempts to stem the tide.

Early on, Walker approached Bob Doyle, Assistant General Manager for Land Acquisitions with the East Bay Regional Park District. Walker requested that the Park District purchase the Marshall property, the place where Walker had been captivated by the deep red color of the manzanitas.

Doyle told him it couldn't be done; there wasn't enough money in the District budget to buy more land.

In response, Walker asked Doyle what he should do. Doyle said he needed to convince people that they should care about a patch of land 'way off in the distance, maybe someplace most of them would never actually visit. And so it began.

Time after time, Walker presented his slideshow to just about anybody who would have him. In hearings and community meetings, with the Boy Scouts, Kiwanis clubs, and local officials, he lobbied, reasoned, cajoled, and appealed – then did it all over again.

When Walker learned that hundreds of houses were planned for Pleasanton Ridge, along with an 18-hole golf course, he began introducing new visitors to Pleasanton Ridge.

Rain or shine, every Saturday for several months he would lead hikers along the ridgeline, pointing out sights along the way, "large old magnificent oaks, beautiful meadowed spots, wonderful sycamores, and rather surprising views of Pleasanton down below and into the distance."

At the end of every hike Walker would ask participants to fill out one of the prepaid, pre-addressed postcards that he just happened to be carrying. Each card encouraged the East Bay Regional Park District to acquire Pleasanton Ridge once and for all as an official park.

Slowly, very slowly, like a great ocean liner attempting to avoid a collision, the tide of public opinion began to turn.

Walker led many weekend hikes to draw the public into his campaign to preserve Pleasanton Ridge. Of course at the end of each hike, he insisted that every hiker then write postcards to public officials advocating preservation.

The ridge was finally saved only at the last minute when one independent-minded owner sold his land to the Park District rather than to the developers. He wasn't a friend by any means but he liked the developers even less. It turned out they'd printed a brochure showing his property in the midst of 2300 homes as the 14th green of their planned golf course – before they'd even talked to him.

Bob Doyle, Assistant General Manager for Land Acquisitions, East Bay Regional Park District

Pleasanton Ridge

Pleasanton Ridge Regional Park
West of Pleasanton, California
April 1985

Looking west across Pleasanton Ridge Regional Park of the East Bay Regional Park District, Pleasanton Ridge itself appears in the east toward the bottom of this view, with Sunol Ridge to the west across the top and Sinbad Canyon running north and south between the two.

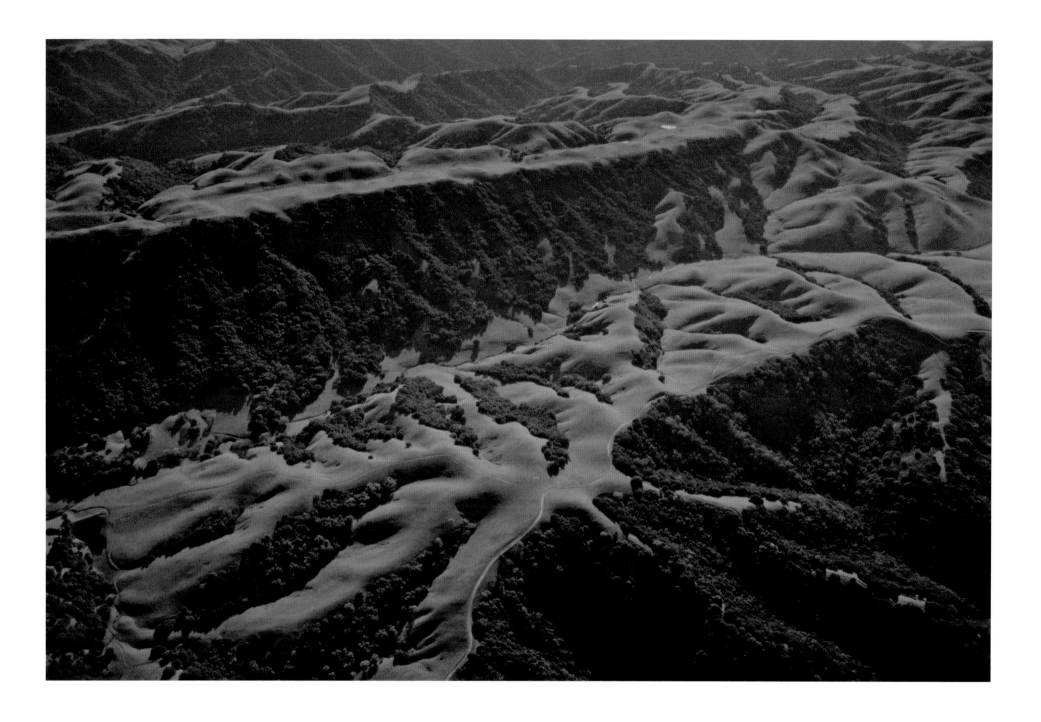

Apperson Ridge Trees

Nipper Ranch
Now Pleasant Ridge Regional Park
West of Pleasanton, California
January 1985

One can hear the leaves rustle in this image of backlit trees from Pleasanton Ridge. A simple enough picture, and yet one almost feels like lying down on the rough grass of the ridgetop to drink it all in.

From photo to photo, Walker's compositions consistently seem to achieve a sense of balance and harmony, always with close attention paid to time of day and quality of light.

Sometimes the viewer's pleasure lies simply in the encounter with another Walker photograph, a delight in the way he viewed the world.

Finally, as in this image, analysis matters less and less the longer one looks.

One simply begins to take pleasure in the sense of what it might have felt like to stand alongside Walker in this same grove of trees on an unseasonably warm afternoon in January.

It would have been one of those days when the air feels perfect – fresh and clear; the earth is dry enough to take a walk; a day when you've got all the time in the world and enough peace of mind to enjoy it.

Moss-Covered Trees

West of Pleasanton, California
November 1985

Deep in the heart of Pleasanton Ridge Regional Park lies Sinbad Canyon along Kilcare Creek, west of Sunol Ridge. Bathed in a thick mossy green this image quietly attests to what much of the East Bay might have looked like in the absence of grazing cattle.

Hillsides and valleys remain thick with uncropped underbrush. Groves of trees with varying thicknesses and heights indicate that young trees are allowed to grow rather than being shorn by passing cattle.

In the years since Walker began leading his weekend hikes, all of the upper Sinbad Creek watershed has been purchased and preserved by the East Bay Regional Park District: all of the slopes, tributaries, and ridgetops that funnel the surrounding rainfall into the creek.

It was a unique time when I got to know Bob Walker, a time when we managed to save the best of the last. I still remember vividly there were three or four major landfill debates, meaning fights over where to build garbage dumps, "the Dump Wars" as we called them.

Round Valley itself was supposed to be a dump, and Marsh Canyon next to it and the Garaventa/Black Diamond Dump, and one on C&H property they owned in the hills above Carquinez Strait. And the Park District ended up acquiring all of the land in question, except Marsh Creek; but even there the garbage dump was defeated largely because Bob Walker was on the case with his photographs and his postcards.

The challenge and the opportunity to protect what's left is every bit as great as it was then, maybe even more important now since we're seeing the last surviving tracts of open space continue to dwindle.

Bob Doyle, Assistant General Manager for Land Acquisition, East Bay Regional Park District

Round Valley

Round Valley Regional Preserve
Near Brentwood, California
April 1987

Round Valley was sold to the East Bay Regional Park District in 1988 by the James Murphy family to protect the land from development as a garbage dump.

One stormy day in 1983 while exploring a remote area near Mount Diablo, Walker felt his photography connect with the landscape more fully than ever before. He watched a patch of hazy light drift across the valley below, and realized that the sun would soon break through the clouds to illuminate a nearby ridge. "It was the first time I actually conceived a potential photograph rather than just reacting," he later remembered of what would become his favorite photograph.

Walker, who often described himself as just a guy looking for a place to walk his dog, was magnetic and exuberant and he loved the land. Through his photography, he captured the richness of the open countryside that he felt so acutely. He used his photographs to convey the urgency of preserving this land for the benefit of everyone rather than allowing it to become the private domain of the few. In the process, the weekend photographer became an artist.

Sarah Pollock, Professor of Journalism, Mills College

Winter Clouds over Marsh Creek

Marshall, Perry, and Cardoza Properties
Morgan Territory Regional Preserve
and Mount Diablo State Park
North of Livermore, California
February 1983

In gently rolling hills once proposed for development as "ranchettes," Walker took this pivotal photo. It signaled not only a milestone in his artistic development, but marked the beginning of his transition from weekend hiker to environmental activist.

When the photograph was taken in early 1983, with the exception of Mount Diablo in the far distance to the north in the upper right corner and the land immediately beneath his feet, the entire landscape arrayed before Walker remained in private hands.

In 1988, Walker used this image and others like it to support a landmark and ultimately successful campaign to pass Measure AA, a $225 million land preservation bond issue. Seth Adams of Save Mount Diablo called Walker "AA's biggest cheerleader."

Passed by East Bay voters, the measure gave the East Bay Regional Park District funds to triple the size of Morgan Territory, among many other acquisitions. Bob Doyle's challenge that Walker use his photographs to make people care about open space had been fulfilled.

As a result of Walker's efforts and a great deal of ongoing work by many others, every inch of land in Walker's emerald image has now been preserved, some added to Mount Diablo State Park, the rest as additions to Morgan Territory Regional Preserve.

Instead of ranchettes for the few, Walker's protected open space continues to welcome the golden eagles and cloud formations whose shadows grace the glowing ridgetops.

There are wonderful areas where the streams do still flow. And the wildflowers go through their cycles. As the landscape changes, perhaps the only thing that might change is the seasons from our golden summers to our stormy green winters.

Bob Walker slideshow

Marsh Creek Cascades

Morgan Territory Regional Preserve
Southeast of Brentwood, California
March 1984

Contemplating this cool, shaded bend, one can easily imagine the many voices of the water as it courses across the exposed rock. The first drops of Marsh Creek originate in Walker's beloved Morgan Territory Regional Preserve while the creek's outlet passes through another park, Big Break Regional Shoreline, at the eastern boundary of the Park District.

Since the time of what Walker and others called "the Dump Wars," one parcel of land after another was preserved. The Park District has now acquired 7 of the 30 miles comprising Marsh Creek, once and perhaps yet again, a vital habitat for spawning salmon.

131

Vasco Caves is a place of stories. Some handed down in spoken word from generation to generation. Others inscribed in stone. Within the shallow sandstone hollows of Vasco Caves lie hidden treasures, pictographs and petroglyphs left by the first inhabitants of the East Bay.

To the people of the Miwok, Ohlone, and Yokut, the Vasco Caves site was kept apart from all but their most spiritual guardians. Only they or those under their guidance were permitted to come face to face with the painted and carved images that rest on the walls of the caves.

In terms of open space and endangered species preservation, Bob Doyle of the East Bay Park District has called Vasco one of the "best and most important wild places left in the East Bay."

Vasco Caves and the surrounding land were preserved through funding from a series of public agencies: California State Parks; Contra Costa Water District; and Wildlife Conservation Board.

Additions to the original preserve were purchased by the East Bay Regional Park District with private funds from the Gordon and Betty Moore Foundation, an offshoot of the Intel success story. More than 1300 acres in total have been protected.

To visit, contact the District to join one of their guided tours, the only access permitted to this sacred site.

Vasco Caves

Vasco Caves Regional Preserve
Northeast of Livermore, California
February 1988

Vasco Caves Interior

Vasco Caves Regional Preserve
Northeast of Livermore, California
February 1988

As visitors to the caves had done since the beginning of time, Walker turned from the interior view toward the light, and the dry chaparral that lies below.

Out of respect for the traditions associated with the engravings and paintings found on the walls of Vasco Caves, none of these images has been reproduced in this collection.

The sacred art of Vasco Caves remains reserved for those who visit with respect, to be gazed upon with thoughts for the people who came before, and for all those who enter the caves in a spirit of reverence.

Vernal Pool

Los Vaqueros Reservoir Watershed
Adjacent to Vasco Caves Regional Preserve
North of Livermore, California
February 1988

The area surrounding Vasco Caves is equally to be honored. It harbors one of the true miracles of life: the habitat of vernal pools.

Touched by winter's rain, from the dust of summer comes life. For these circular ponds come into being only when it rains. No stream feeds the stone basins nor do porous rocks allow them to empty. They are habitats unto themselves.

As the pools form, several endangered species, among them longhorn fairy shrimp, reappear on the otherwise barren rock.

During the rest of the year, the pools dry to powder and dust. Somehow the endangered species survive in the absolute absence of water . . . until the rains return and the pools once again fill with life.

The wind-tossed slopes on which Walker stood to photograph Miller/Knox Regional Shoreline are renowned for kite-flying and birdwatching.

To San Francisco Bay swimmers, the "frozen chosen," as they like to characterize themselves, Miller/Knox harbors Keller's Beach, off to the right beyond the reach of Walker's lens, one of the relatively "warmer" swimming locales along the bay.

To the upper right jutting into the bay, Ferry Point recalls a time before the Bay and Golden Gate bridges, for this was the western terminus of the transcontinental railroad completed in 1869. From there until the 1950s, ferry boats conveyed passengers and freight to San Francisco, whose high-rise towers can be seen in the distance.

Named for two open space advocates, Representative George Miller and member of the state assembly John Knox, the shoreline park owes an equal debt to other citizen activists, among them Jay and Barbara Vincent, along with Lucretia Edwards (1916–2005) and her husband, Thomas.

Reportedly, Lucretia Edwards burst into tears when she learned that portions of the hillsides were to be developed as high-rise apartments. In response, her husband cashed in his pension and bought the land for her as a gift, the foundation for what later became Miller/Knox Regional Shoreline.

Miller/Knox Regional Shoreline

West and adjacent to Point Richmond, California
March 1988

A view of the East Bay's shoreline as it might have appeared before the coming of the Europeans. Point Isabel takes its name from the favorite daughter of Vicente Castro, the first person to hold written title to the land now occupied by Point Isabel Regional Shoreline.

Immediately before us lies Point Isabel's Hoffman Marsh and a barely glimpsed San Francisco Bay Trail at water's edge. An important habitat for nesting birds, low-lying, petite Brooks Island Regional Shoreline can be found offshore and farther to the south.

At the time of the 1849 Gold Rush, nearly 200,000 acres of similar land bordered San Francisco Bay. Only about 30,000 acres remain largely due to filling of the bay's marshes, mudflats, and formerly underwater shoreline areas for use as garbage dumps, airports, and housing as well as for use by the military.

This practice was formally stopped by legislation in 1965 through the efforts of Save the Bay, formed four years earlier by three women: Esther Gulick, Kay Kerr, and Sylvia McLaughlin.

Some believe the actions of the three women played a major role in the Bay Area's modern environmental movement, a turning point as important as Rosa Parks' refusal to move to the back of the bus was to civil rights.

Point Isabel, known as the friendliest off-leash dog park in the nation – over a million visitors per year, not including their owners – also offers protected and secluded habitat for the rarest of the rare among the region's birds, the reclusive and endangered clapper rail.

Point Isabel and Marina Bay

Point Isabel Regional Shoreline
West of Richmond, California
May 1988

Walker here records the influx of high tide at Breuner Marsh. In the middle distance railroad tracks cut horizontally through the landscape separating the marsh from the housing of Parchester Village beyond. When World War II ended, Parchester became the first housing development in the Bay Area open to African Americans.

Years passed. The marsh, sometimes called Parchester Marsh by local residents, remained much the same as it had always been. The owner, a family member of the man who founded Breuner Furniture, left the land alone: pure open space, not protected but not developed either.

One adjoining piece of property became a rod and gun club while another evolved into an airfield for model airplanes. Both continue to hold their ground. Casual strolls into the southern edge of Breuner marsh often take place against an audio backdrop of gunshots and buzzing motors.

Whatever the surrounding uses, many Parchester residents regarded the marsh, in the words of their website, www.eastshorepark.org, as "the environmental heart of our historic black community."

Over time, the Park District also recognized the field as an important ecological niche, one of the last undeveloped and unprotected stretches of coastal marsh and upland prairie along the entire coast of San Francisco Bay.

In contrast, the owners who bought the land from Breuner saw the potential for real estate development. With the marsh appropriately filled and security established, the land could then play host to a bevy of bayshore condominiums.

Both for its ecological importance as well as the key role this open space and shoreline access offers as recreation for the surrounding urban neighborhoods, the District wanted to add the marsh to Pinole Regional Shoreline.

After negotiations with the most recent private owners of the marsh broke down, the Park District took legal action to acquire all but 20 acres of the property.

Praising the District's response, Whitney Dotson, President of the Parchester Neighborhood Council, was quoted in the *Contra Costa Times* as declaring, "This has been 56 years in the making; the Park District really represented us well on this one. It's been a long, long struggle."

Nearby residents and visitors alike will forever be able to wander through a mix of marsh and coastal grassland that shows what the Bay Area looked like when the Ohlone and Yokut inhabited its flanks, when Gaspar de Portolá first realized that San Francisco Bay existed, and when Parchester Village came into being in 1949.

Breuner Marsh

Now part of Point Pinole Regional Shoreline
West of Richmond, California
May 1988

Walker once explained that he finally understood how the clapper rail became endangered: "I almost stepped on it three times trying to take its picture and it never moved once."

Eventually photographed by Walker at a more comfortable distance, the clapper rail seen opposite at water's edge does indeed wait motionless hoping to escape detection. The rail's patience is further assisted by its helpful disguise, a rusty gray coloring that matches the pickleweed and cordgrass of the shoreline marshes.

Thanks to preservation efforts, the numbers of clapper rail in the Bay area have risen from a low of 300 in 1990 to a total of perhaps 1200, if one includes all the marshes of San Francisco Bay.

California Clapper Rail

Palo Alto Baylands Nature Preserve
East of Palo Alto, California
February 1989

Fishing at Wilson Point

San Pablo Bay Regional Shoreline
West of Richmond, California
November 1987

The ancient art of fishing lives on! Where shoals of mussels once covered shoreline rocks and oyster beds grew thick enough to attract oyster pirates like the young Jack London, two fishing friends maintain an age-old agreement with the open water of the bay.

The importance of this image to Walker was evidenced by those who transferred his photographic archive from Walker's home to the Oakland Museum. Left on his light table, it was among those being edited for a future slideshow at the time of Walker's death.

The property lines of the United States survey that radiated from Mount Diablo divided the marshland of the East Bay into private property that could be bought and sold in an orderly and controlled manner.

From the time of the Gold Rush on, the shoreline, once teeming with wildlife and hunting grounds for the Bay Area's first inhabitants, was too often considered a wasteland, best suited for garbage dumps and industry.

In 1892, Point Pinole became the site of the Giant Company, a manufacturer of the explosives invented by Alfred Nobel. On more than one occasion the surrounding hills of the shoreline grumbled with accidental explosions.

Closed as a dynamite factory in 1960, the first parcels of Point Pinole Regional Shoreline were purchased by the Park District in 1971. The detonations had been replaced by silence and as noted in this tranquil Walker image, serenity.

Point Pinole Twilight

Point Pinole Regional Shoreline
West of Richmond, California
November 1987

CHAPTER SEVEN

The Delta and Beyond

Wild fowl, quacking hordes of them, nest in the tulares [meaning, tule reeds]. All day wings beat above it hazy with speed; long flights of cranes glimmer in the twilight. By night one wakes to hear the clanging geese go over. What they do there, how fare, what find, is the secret of the tulares.

Mary Austin, *Land of Little Rain* (1903)

Delta Tule Reeds

Delta of the Sacramento and San Joaquin rivers
East of Antioch, California
West of Sacramento, California
March 1990

The Delta and Beyond

As the 1980s came to an end, Walker broadened his concerns into statewide water issues. From the East Bay he ventured farther eastward from the lands surrounding Mount Diablo.

Commissions from those who increasingly recognized his skill, among them the East Bay Regional Park District, directed Walker toward the northern shores of San Francisco Bay and inland along the Carquinez Strait to the east of Mount Diablo. Beyond Carquinez, and to the west, lies Suisun Bay and then one of the world's great deltas, akin to the Nile, the Mekong, the Okavango, the Amazon.

As he pursued this new direction, Walker entered a much-altered landscape once dominated by marsh and tule reeds. Vast stands of these hollow grasslike reeds, moving in tune with the ancient rhythms of tide, wind, and current, were far more characteristic of the historic Delta than the farmland and waterways of today.

The word *tule* itself is ancient. It originated in the long ago time of the Aztecs and thence from the Spanish, where the word *tulares* translates as tule reeds. The California town of Tulare takes its name from the once lush, now almost extinct tule marshes of the Central Valley.

Through the Delta's labyrinth of levees and waterways flow California's two great rivers, the Sacramento and the San Joaquin, on their way to San Francisco Bay and the Pacific Ocean.

As they enter the Delta, the two rivers change shape, spreading into meandering channels and sloughs: the central pivot point for the largest water system ever constructed on earth.

Half the water that falls on the state of California finds its way into the Delta. Its waters irrigate nearly 5 million acres of farmland and support the world's sixth largest economy. Siphoned by gigantic electrical pumps, fresh water from the Delta supplies fresh drinking water for 24 million people as far away as Los Angeles and San Diego.

Two-thirds of the state's salmon migrate through its tangle of artificial islands and their protective 1000 miles of levees. Half the waterfowl that nest along the Pacific Coast of North America do so in the Delta's marshes and wetlands.

In what would be some of Walker's final projects, he turned his attention to what were then some of the newer parks in the East Bay Regional Park system and even to areas well outside the Park District's reach.

Water issues became prominent: preservation of both land and water-based habitat; the dilemma of the aging levees; and more broadly the nature of human intervention on the land. In so doing Walker documented landscape issues that would increasingly come to the forefront in this fragile and little known landscape. For the fate of the Delta is the fate of California.

Port Costa and the Carquinez Strait

Carquinez Strait Regional Shoreline
Port Costa, California
November 1985

Carquinez Strait Regional Shoreline lies on the near shore as a work-in-progress regional park. Individual parcels of land have been set aside by the East Bay Regional Park District, while encroaching suburban housing developments have already begun marking the hills to the north.

This also marks the transition point where the northern end of San Francisco Bay gives way first to San Pablo Bay, then Suisun Bay, and finally leads onward to the Delta of the Sacramento and San Joaquin rivers.

In what appears to be an aerial photograph, Walker directs the viewer's eye north across Black Diamond Mines Regional Preserve of the East Bay Regional Park District toward the city of Pittsburg. Instead of hovering above the landscape, Walker actually had his feet firmly planted on the northern peak of Mount Diablo.

Small, geographically important Sherman Island appears to the right as a thin brown triangle in the horizontal flow of water. The islands to the left, west of Sherman Island, are Winter Island in the middle, sometimes called "Winters Island," and Browns Island Regional Preserve all the way to the west.

As the 19th century drew to a close, Winter Island became home to an idealistic, communally owned utopian society. By 1901 the community had passed into history. Some members remained and the island reverted to private farmland.

Later, the island served as a private duck-hunting club and disposal site for mud dredged elsewhere for levee and marina maintenance by the United States Army Corps of Engineers.

Despite the island's checkered history, portions of its land today remain a tule-covered habitat for birds, beaver, and muskrats.

While the story of Winter Island is not uncommon in the Delta, Browns Island Regional Shoreline, on the other hand, is an especially rare piece of the labyrinth. Its 595 acres survive as a virtually untouched remnant of the original landscape.

The island remains without levees and above water level – no small accomplishments in the heavily managed Delta – nor does it offer guest facilities or so much as a visitor's center. However, it does make for some tremendously undisturbed opportunities to explore the island and nearby sloughs by kayak or canoe.

At the western tip of Sherman Island, California's two largest rivers end their long journeys from the Sierra Nevada: the 380-mile-long Sacramento River flowing from the north on the far side of the island, and the 320-mile-long San Joaquin River entering from the south.

The merging rivers enter what is officially known as Suisun Bay. The strong current of fresh water continues eastward through Carquinez Strait and onward through the Golden Gate. The constant interchange of fresh water flowing into the ocean and salty ocean water flooding inward with the tide, forms the ecological basis of the Delta, San Francisco Bay, and influences the coastal waters of the Pacific Ocean.

Pittsburg and Sherman Island

Looking north from Mount Diablo
Across Black Diamond Mines Regional Preserve
Pittsburg, California
August 1984

Natural and artificial river channels mark an expansive floodplain in this view looking west toward the lowering sun of a late afternoon and a far distant San Francisco Bay.

In this one image, Walker encapsulates 150 years of human intervention in the landscape.

Boat channels have been dredged in straight parallel lines along both sides of the ecologically sound S curves of the original sloughs and river channels, or simply cut straight through existing meanders.

Neat lines of crops mark farmland that rests 3 to 21 feet below the level of the surrounding water, preserved from flooding by fragile and aging levees.

Many fear that the Delta and the 550,000 acres of farmland unfolding beneath our flight pattern is on the verge of catastrophic collapse, from earthquake or flood, perhaps on a scale beyond any hope of recovery or reconstruction.

The names given to many of the 60 artificial islands found in the Delta reflect an earlier generation's more innocent dreams for the so-called reclaimed land of Delta farms: Empire Tract; Venice Island; and the drowned island now appearing as a lake toward the center horizon, Frank's Tract, flooded in 1938.

The California Department of Fish and Game's White Slough Wildlife Area, an important nesting area for ducks and geese, lies below the twin oxbow bends that outline King Island, left, and Empire Tract, right. South of the oxbows, Disappointment Slough offers an east-west side channel north of the San Joaquin River.

From here the San Joaquin continues its westward journey to its rendezvous with the Sacramento River at Sherman Island.

The combined waters then flow through Suisun Bay, Carquinez Strait, and along the northern edge of the East Bay Regional Park District.

Delta, San Joaquin River and Sacramento River

Southwest of Sacramento, California
April 1989

A meditative ground-level view of White Slough and the White Slough Wildlife Area north of King Island, the same landscape seen from the air on the previous page.

Taken on a chilly winter's day as the last touch of sunlight slips from sight, this would be one of Walker's final photographs.

Delta Slough Sunset

Southwest of Sacramento, California
February 1991

CHAPTER EIGHT

Day is Done

San Antonio Wildflowers

Private land along Mines Road
East of San Jose, California and Mount Hamilton
April 1985

Day is Done

In 1992, near the end of Walker's life, a friend asked him if there was anything else he wanted to do, anything to see or photograph, anywhere in the world. Without a pause, Walker answered no, there wasn't. He'd done what he needed to do. His work had been completed.

Walker did say, however, that he would like to see the wild-flowers of San Antonio Valley one more time. There'd been a good rain after a dry spell; he knew it would be a great year for wildflowers, especially in San Antonio Valley, the fields he'd photographed from the beginning. Let's take a look, he said.

And then, after lying on his back bathed in a seemingly endless field of blossoms . . . that visit, too, had been completed.

I'd sit with the dog and watch the light dance on the hills around Diablo and dream a very special dream. Wouldn't it be nice, I thought, if instead of miles of private land and subdivision threats, all the land between Morgan Territory and these beautiful foothills were ours as permanently protected public land.

Bob Walker

Taken in Morgan Territory Regional Preserve overlooking Riggs Canyon whose protection Walker helped safeguard, with the snowcapped twin peaks of Mount Diablo beyond.

What had been a small, isolated 930-acre preserve when Walker first hiked its ridges and hills now stretches in an unbroken line that connects Morgan Territory Regional Preserve with Mount Diablo State Park.

Here one can witness the greatest population of golden eagles in all the world. Here one could rest assured that open space in all directions would be preserved for all time, a place to walk without fear that the land would be turned under for houses and malls.

In the end, Walker had achieved much of his dream: that one day Morgan Territory would be protected, that there would be many places where "a guy could find a place to walk his dog."

When Walker first began his career as an environmental activist, Morgan Territory was a small, isolated regional park separated on the east from Mount Diablo State Park by more than 5 miles of private land holdings.

Today, Morgan Territory has been connected to the state park by an open-space corridor collaboratively acquired by Save Mount Diablo, the State of California, and the East Bay Regional Park District. As Walker said after this goal had been achieved, "Never hesitate to dream."

In all, Walker has been credited with making key contributions to the creation of Eastshore State Park, Pleasanton Ridge Regional Park, Round Valley Regional Preserve, and of course, the expansion of Morgan Territory. The 1988 passage of Bond Measure AA, which Walker tirelessly championed, funded expansion of the Park District from 60,000 acres to more than 97,000 acres of protected open space.

Shortly before Walker's death, the East Bay Regional Park District acknowledged the sum of Walker's remarkable accomplishments. The District gave Walker's name to a ridge and a new trail in Walker's favorite Morgan Territory.

In return, Walker deemed the Park District's recognition "the greatest honor of my life."

Bob Walker Self-Portrait

Morgan Territory Regional Preserve
Southwest of Brentwood, California
February 1990

The lesson is quite clear: by joining the knowledge and talents of everyone, weekend hikers, armchair enthusiasts, average citizens and environmental leaders, old groups and new, we can prevail.

Bob Walker

Valley Oak at Dusk

Pleasanton Ridge Regional Park
West of Pleasanton, California
June 1985

On private property when originally photographed by Walker, this magnificent valley oak stands on land that became part of Pleasanton Ridge Regional Park. Later additions significantly extended the park south toward the town of Sunol and west toward Hayward.

With its promise of new growth and regeneration after the storms of winter, the embracing branches of this magnificent oak served as the traditional conclusion for many of Walker's slideshows.

Their sculptural grace serves here as a hallmark of Bob Walker's photographic art.

Their continued existence turn stands as a crowning testament to everything Walker accomplished and the many lessons he leaves behind – acknowledged with gratitude by everyone who has ever experienced, or will experience, the bountiful wonder of the East Bay Regional Park District.

ADDITIONAL INFORMATION

People and Places

About the East Bay Regional Park District

From its inception in 1934, the East Bay Regional Park District has grown to encompass 65 parks with 29 regional trails running some 1100 miles across 97,000 acres of land throughout the East Bay, covering the counties of Alameda and Contra Costa.

The surprisingly varied names given to the parks bear witness to the range of the District's responsibilities: *regional parks* indicate large protected areas with multiple uses; *regional preserves* define areas of intrinsic cultural, historical, and biological value; *regional recreation areas* highlight activities such as hiking and swimming; *regional shorelines* safeguard water, land, and tidal areas along San Francisco Bay, San Pablo Bay, and the Sacramento/San Joaquin Delta. *Regional trails* provide pedestrian, horseback, and bicycle connections with other parks and communities.

On this map we have highlighted in dark green the parks where Bob Walker stood to make the photographs in this book.

Starting with personal photography, and later under contract with the East Bay Regional Park District and other groups, Walker documented many other parks within the Park District.

In addition, Walker photographed many parcels of land that fell outside the District's boundaries, land that he and others dreamed of preserving. In that sense, Walker continues to point visitors and viewers alike toward the land left to be preserved and protected by those who follow in his footsteps.

All of these images and those Walker took during his photographic apprenticeship in the High Sierra and American Southwest are available to the public through the Bob Walker Photography Collection at the Natural Sciences Department, Oakland Museum of California in Oakland, California. See page 176 for additional information on the images in this book.

A complete guide to the East Bay Regional Park District, including many organized public activities, can be found on the Internet at www.ebparks.org. The website includes detailed descriptions of individual parks, including histories, maps, hiking trails, educational activities, and additional visitor information. One special note: information and reservations for guided tours of Vasco Caves Regional Park, the only public access permitted, may be made by calling (510) 636-1684 or (888) 327-2757.

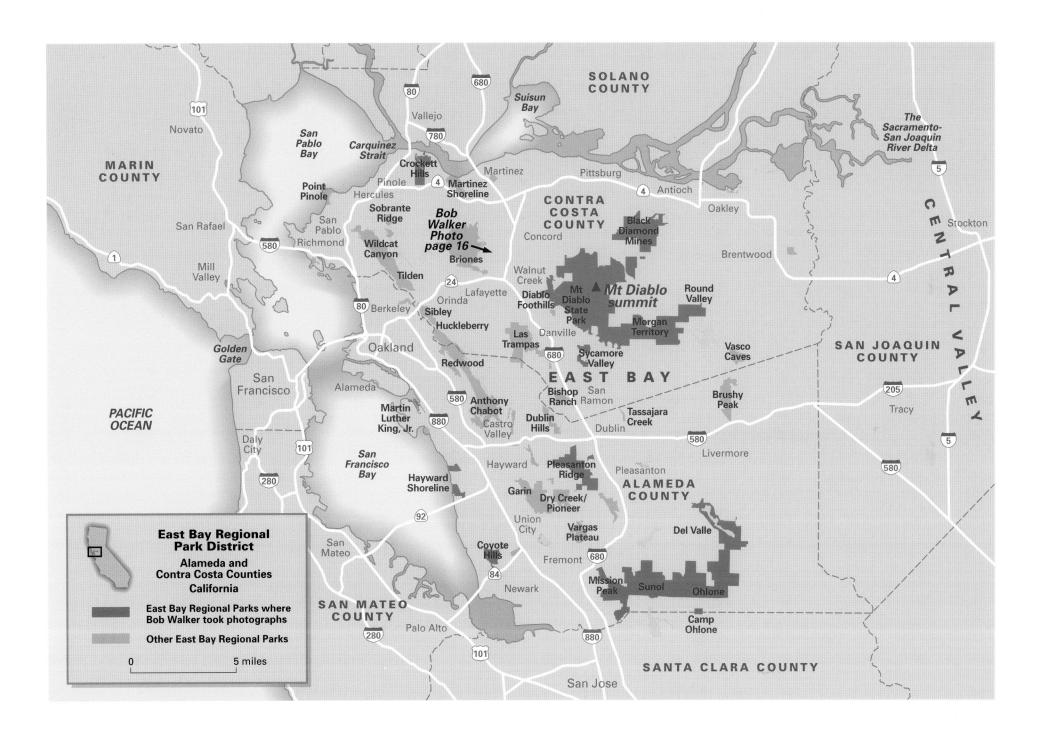

MARIN
COUNTY

Novato

San
Pablo
Bay

SOLANO
COUNTY

Suisun
Bay

The
Sacramento-
San Joaquin
River Delta

Vallejo

Carquinez
Strait

San Rafael

Point
Pinole

Pinole
Hercules

Crockett
Hills

Martinez

Martinez
Shoreline

Pittsburg

Antioch

Oakley

Stockton

Mill
Valley

San
Pablo
Richmond

Sobrante
Ridge

Bob
Walker
Photo
page 16

Briones

CONTRA
COSTA
COUNTY

Concord

Black
Diamond
Mines

Brentwood

Wildcat
Canyon

Walnut
Creek

C E N T R A L   V A L L E Y

Tilden

Orinda

Lafayette

Golden
Gate

San
Francisco

Berkeley

Sibley

Huckleberry

Oakland

Alameda

Redwood

Diablo
Foothills

Mt
Diablo
State
Park

Mt Diablo
summit

Round
Valley

Morgan
Territory

SAN JOAQUIN
COUNTY

Las
Trampas

Danville

Sycamore
Valley

Vasco
Caves

E A S T   B A Y

PACIFIC
OCEAN

Martin
Luther
King, Jr.

Anthony
Chabot

Bishop
Ranch

San
Ramon

Brushy
Peak

Tracy

Daly
City

Castro
Valley

Dublin
Hills

Tassajara
Creek

Dublin

Livermore

San
Francisco
Bay

Hayward
Shoreline

Hayward

Pleasanton
Ridge

Pleasanton

ALAMEDA
COUNTY

San
Mateo

Garin

Dry Creek/
Pioneer

Del Valle

Union
City

Vargas
Plateau

SAN MATEO
COUNTY

Coyote
Hills

Fremont

Newark

Mission
Peak

Sunol

Ohlone

Camp
Ohlone

Palo Alto

SANTA CLARA COUNTY

San Jose

East Bay Regional Park District

Alameda and Contra Costa Counties California

East Bay Regional Parks where Bob Walker took photographs

Other East Bay Regional Parks

0   5 miles

Many hikes are possible in this splendid park land; the one described below takes in the widest range of wonders, with optional side trips along the way.

Allow four hours minimum, more for enjoying the sights along the way. An easier hike with much less up and down can be made by staying on the [Volvon Trail] ridge trails [former ranch roads] instead of turning left at (2) to descend into the canyon.

(1) Parking Lot, Water. (2) At the top of the first hill, take a left turn [Coyote Trail] just past the fence, go steeply down the hill along the fence, cross the small stream, and up to the meadow beyond. (3) You can begin here to descend into the canyon, but don't miss the chance to go out to viewpoint (4) for the best view of Marsh Creek Canyon.

From (3) [Condor Trail], contour around the hill on one of several cow paths, turn left on a vague path just over the crest of the ridge, and continue to the end of the ridge. Enjoy the view and a great picnic spot. Return to (3) and begin a steep descent into the canyon on cow paths that eventually resolve into one trail that takes you the rest of the way along this glorious stream.

(5) At the point where the main fork can be seen coming down the hill from the left, a short side trip up its steep streambed will bring you to a beautiful series of pools and cascades edged by ferns and mosses.

As you continue beyond (5), various wonders unfold: meadows dotted with old oaks, splashing side streams, and Marsh Creek itself. Stay along the stream until (6). The trail turns right though a low gap and quickly enters wide, open meadows. There is no obvious trail continuing downstream [out of the park] from this point so don't worry about missing the turn.

[Continue west across the road and into the new additions to the preserve.]

(7) At a group of rocks to the left of the trail, several grinding holes can be seen. Using a rock pestle, the Indians of Marsh Creek ground acorns into flour in these rounded mortars.

(8) A long but beautiful walk up the hill along an old ranch road brings you eventually to a junction with the main ridge road [Volvon Trail]. Turn right to return to the parking lot or continue north along the [Bob Walker] ridge to another "shouldn't be missed" viewpoint.

(9) Leave the road at the height of the land and walk out a short distance on the path to (10), at the park's northern boundary. From here you look out across a series of beautiful ridges toward the San Joaquin River, the Delta, and on a clear day, the snowcapped High Sierra across the vast flat Central Valley. [The parallel ridges below were the proposed site of a ranchette housing project that Bob helped defeat; they descend

into large, flat Round Valley, which Walker also helped preserve.]

The canyon on the left is not Marsh Creek, but Sycamore Canyon [which remains outside the Preserve].

(10) Head back south along the [Bob Walker] ridge on roads to either side [Volvon Loop], or head overland along its windswept top for the views. After the roads rejoin, don't miss the view from the open grassy ridge just west of the road (11). Numerous cow paths and foot trails can be followed to the mystical spots that abound along the ridge. Dotted lines roughly mark a couple of favorites near (12).

(13) From the open meadow where one old farm implement and several picnic tables can be seen, you can pick your way through the brush to the west to the tops of the cliffs – shown as a dotted line [Prairie Falcon Trail]. Continue south along the road, bearing right at the meadow where several roads join. After passing though a gap between two hills, you enter yet another open meadow.

Before heading right up the hill and back to the parking lot take a side trip to (14), where amongst the rocks there are more grinding holes than any other spot I've seen in the Bay Area. This is the site of a splendid Native American village that sat where the headwaters divide into streams running north and south. A 'family-sized'

Indian cave can be found in the trees on the side of the hill at (15). A grinding hole can be found in the flat rock 'table' outside the overhang.

With any luck, all of this has made some kind of sense and you've successfully found your way back to your car. And if you've come under the spell of this mystical place, you're no doubt planning a quick return. Enjoy!

* * *

After Bob Walker's death on September 19, 1992, among his papers, we discovered this unpublished hiking guide to Morgan Territory that he'd written in 1986. Several features have changed since Bob wrote his original descriptions. We've added bracketed notations to keep you on track.

When Bob led his hikes in Morgan Territory, at the end of the day just before everybody returned home, he'd always ask participants to write a note to the Board of Directors, East Bay Regional Park District, P.O. Box 5381, Oakland, CA 94605. In that note, Bob encouraged everyone to thank the board for their efforts to protect the preserve, and to request funding for further expansion. We hope you'll do the same.

Seth Adams
Director of Land Programs
Save Mount Diablo

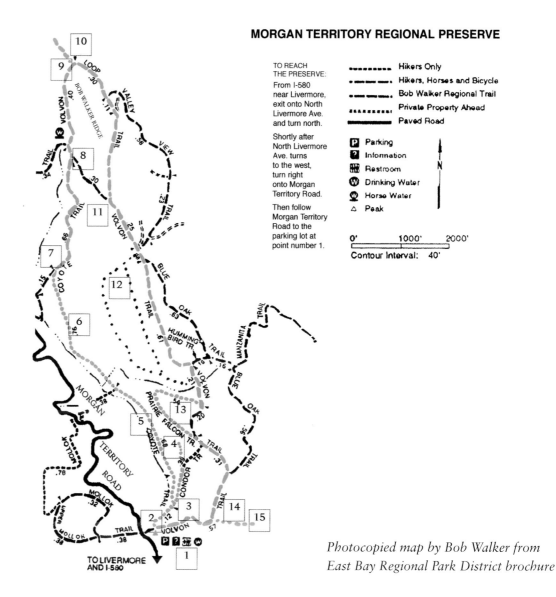

MORGAN TERRITORY REGIONAL PRESERVE

TO REACH
THE PRESERVE:
From I-580 near Livermore, exit onto North Livermore Ave. and turn north.

Shortly after North Livermore Ave. turns to the west, turn right onto Morgan Territory Road.

Then follow Morgan Territory Road to the parking lot at point number 1.

- - - - - - - Hikers Only
- · - · - · Hikers, Horses and Bicycle
- — · — · Bob Walker Regional Trail
· · · · · · · · Private Property Ahead
▬▬▬▬ Paved Road

🅿 Parking
❓ Information
🚻 Restroom
W Drinking Water
Ⓦ Horse Water
△ Peak

0'   1000'   2000'

Contour Interval: 40'

Photocopied map by Bob Walker from
East Bay Regional Park District brochure

Bob Walker Photography Collection

According to his wishes, Bob Walker's photographic archive of more than 40,000 35mm color slides has been preserved in the collection of the Natural Sciences Department, Oakland Museum of California.

Among the activities generated by the Natural Sciences Department, two annual events are closely tied to public use of open space.

On or about Mother's Day, in May, the Department hosts a show of California wildflowers gathered (let it be noted, with full environmental and ecological sensitivity) by volunteers from around the state. The idea is to present newly cut examples of every wildflower that grows within the state's borders.

Similarly the annual Fungus Fair (in existence for over 30 years) features examples of California mushrooms from every nook, cranny, damp meadow, and forest from north to south. For more information on these and other offerings from the Natural Sciences Department please visit www.museumca.org.

Those wishing to use the Walker Collection should contact Carolyn Rissanen, registrar, Natural Sciences Department, tel: (510) 238-3885. Images in this book can be referenced by page and catalogue number:

Credits and Acknowledgments

After the Storm, Bob Walker and the East Bay Regional Park District was designed by Chris Pichler and Christopher Beaver. Photographic scanning and reference prints by Deryl Clark of ScanArt.

Editorial funding provided by the East Bay Regional Park District, Pat O'Brien, General Manager, with additional support from the Natural Sciences Department, Oakland Museum of California.

Caption and text information supplied by Bob Doyle, Peter Dramer, Roger Epperson, Jerry Kent, Traci Parent, and Mark Taylor, all of the East Bay Regional Park District; David Loeb of *Bay Nature* magazine; Seth Adams, Save Mount Diablo, who also connected the author with the folks who published *After the Storm*; John Woodbury, Napa County Regional Park and Open Space District; David Mathews, Mount Diablo State Park; and Sam Shannon, Tilden Park Golf Course.

Lucille Matthews offered guidance with the identification and lore of Bay Area flowers. Jewel Moulthrop reviewed the text and offered much-appreciated comments and observations. In the final stages of authorship, Denise Zmekhol clarified several design issues. Maya Ishiwata, Dorothy Beaver, and Thomas Beaver provided invaluable advice, inspiration, and support.

Special thanks to Pat O'Brien, General Manager, and Rosemary Cameron, Assistant General Manager, Public Affairs, both of the East Bay Regional Park District, for making the Bob Walker book a reality. Additional assistance provided by Mary Mattingly, Lane Powell, and Nancy Schley, East Bay Regional Park District.

Special thanks also to Tom Steller and Carolyn Rissanen of the Natural Sciences Department, Oakland Museum of California, for their stewardship of the Bob Walker Collection and their efforts on behalf of this book.

Heartfelt appreciation to Gay and Lesbian Sierrans who offered steadfast early support for this project; and to poet Jim Mitchell and photographer Tony Heiderer who first placed cameras in Bob Walker's hands.

A special debt of gratitude must go to Barb Moskowitz who employed Walker as a building manager. Her financial support continued long after Walker began to devote much of his time to photography and open space preservation – all with her full and complete blessing.

Thank you to Roslyn Bullas, managing editor, and Laura Keresty, director of marketing and operations, of Wilderness Press for their immediate and enthusiastic "yes" to the prospect of a Bob Walker book.

Thank you also to Wilderness Press as an institution for many wonderful guide books to open-space activities from here to pretty much everywhere, especially the Wilderness Press guide to hiking trails in the East Bay.

To preserve open space, Walker would direct people to different groups according to each person's individual interests. Among those organizations endorsed by Walker for the preservation of open space, the following would certainly have been singled out:

Bay Area Ridge Trail Council
www.ridgetrail.org, (415) 561-25950;
Greenbelt Alliance
www.greenbelt.org, (415) 543-6771;
Preserve Area Ridgelands Committee
www.ridgelands.org, (925) 447-50115;
Save Mount Diablo
www.savemountdiablo.org, (925) 947-3535;
Save the Bay
www.savesfbay.org, (510) 452-9261;
San Francisco Bay Chapter of the Sierra Club
www.sanfranciscobay.sierraclub.org, (510) 848-0800;

and of course, the *East Bay Regional Park District*
www.ebparks.org, (888) 327-2757.

Photographer Robert John Walker was born in Ohio and moved to San Francisco after graduating from Oberlin College in 1972. In addition to winning awards for his photography and becoming widely published, his photographs and slideshows became important elements in efforts to preserve the natural environment of San Francisco Bay and the East Bay region. Walker, a former head of the San Francisco Bay Chapter of the Sierra Club, died in 1992 at the age of 40.

Author and documentary film producer Christopher Beaver was born and raised in Northern California. His films have won numerous awards including a National Emmy in News and Broadcasting. Topics include: the links between nuclear power and nuclear weapons; San Francisco Bay and the open space that borders the bay; and water policy in an age of global warming. To learn more about Christopher Beaver, please visit www.cbfilms.net.

Bob Walker
Photographed by Sarah Pollock

Christopher Beaver
Photographed by Denise Zmekhol